002151

A Christian Approach
to Transactional Analysis

When God Says YOU'RE OK

Jon Tal Murphree

InterVarsity Press
Downers Grove, Illinois 60515

InterVarsity Press is the book publishing division of Inter-Varsity Christian Fellowship, a student movement active on campus at hundreds of universities, colleges and schools of nursing. For information about local and regional activities, write IVCF, 233 Langdon Street, Madison, WI 53703.

Library of Congress Catalog Card Number: 75-21452
ISBN: 0-87784-716-9

Printed in the United States of America

To
Marisa
our baby daughter
who so lovingly hindered
the writing of this book

CONTENTS

INTRODUCTION

When the seventeenth-century philosopher Leibniz responded to John Locke's *An Essay Concerning Human Understanding,* he entitled his work *New Essays Concerning Human Understanding* and remarked in the preface, "I have thought that it would be a good opportunity . . . to obtain a favorable reception for my thoughts by putting them in such good company."

It is with this same spirit of appreciation that I have attempted a Christian application of the principles so clearly presented in Thomas A. Harris' *I'm OK–You're OK.* While he may or may not wish to identify with my adaptation of his categories to Christian truth, I have seen in his approach a restatement of traditional religious themes in terms understandable to the thought patterns of contemporary man.

Speaking as a physician, Harris has been limited in what he could say authoritatively about the Christian faith. As a clergyman I feel freer to express the Christian message through his structures and to apply those structures to practical Christian living. When I say that much of what Harris states is inadequate, I am not saying it is wrong. It is rather a compliment to Harris that he did not go so far beyond his field of the science of human behavior. Because his book is in the general area of psychology it cannot be said to be a distinctively Christian book, nor was it intended to be. But since all truth in the world is God's truth, elements of God's truth in the world may be adopted for immediate utility without adopting the entire body of Christian truth.

This accounts for the large amount of truth in the other great religions of the world.

The element of truth in *I'm OK–You're OK* is primarily in the realm of human relationships and one's relationship with himself. What is missing from a distinctively Christian standpoint is in the area of one's relationship with God. In *When God Says You're OK* I wish to show how this "vertical" relationship with God adds so much to one's "horizontal" relationships in the world. The personal benefits of Transactional Analysis can become so much greater with the addition of this Christian ingredient.

This book should not be read as a critical evaluation of Harris' book, though points of disagreement should be expected. Rather it should be understood for the most part as an appreciative extension of Harris' principles to a dimension which he was not in a position to elucidate. Though I highly recommend his book for its practical helpfulness, *I'm OK–You're OK* is not prerequisite reading for *When God Says You're OK*.

The most exhilarating experience in the world is to see the transparent joy, the new fulfillment, the repaired human relationships and the changed lives of those who have discovered a quiet and confident relationship with God through Jesus Christ. My profession brings me into contact with an increasing number of these persons day after day. This book is written for those who are interested in investigating the possibilities of a meaningful, intelligent relationship with God in their personal lives and discovering what the daily presence of Christ can do for all their other relationships.

Jon Tal Murphree

1

HOW DO YOU RELATE?

Who is as obnoxious as Irene McIntosh? At times she bristles like a porcupine—at other times she freezes you over like an iceberg. She has driven her husband away, estranged her only child and alienated her neighbors. To the women's club meeting she carries a potato chip on her shoulder as regularly as the new moon, daring anyone to knock it off. Through the years she has cultivated the fine art of switching from a sulky pout to an emotional explosion without even trying. To those who know her best, Irene McIntosh has a hornets' nest for a heart.

Frequently interested neighbors and relatives attempt to relate to her in a meaningful way. But apparently her highest priority in life is to protect her misery by keeping everyone at arm's length.

Not far from Irene McIntosh lives a man whom I kept hearing of as "the finest man in the city." He was over 90, but when I visited him I found Joseph Crenshaw working his garden with a hoe. A deep, gruesome gorge stared at me from the side of his face. Yet, despite the cancer on his cheek, the satisfaction of an abundant life was written across that face. Expression lines around the malignancy marked his face with character. Shafts of light came through his sharp eyes exposing a beautiful life behind that ugly face. With a personality scintillating with brightness, Joseph Crenshaw was open and defenseless. And when he spoke, he made me feel as if I were the most important person in the world to him at the moment.

Joseph Crenshaw is able to relate to others, and Irene McIntosh is not. One can accept himself and the other cannot. For one living is fun in spite of adversity; for the other life is a burden.

The fact that one is a man and the other a woman is only coincidence. The entire race of humans is sandwiched between the Joseph Crenshaws and the Irene McIntoshes, either able or unable to relate. Most of us are somewhere between these two extremes, some of us able to relate in more situations, some in fewer.

One roommate attempts to make the other feel important; the other is on an endless crusade to establish his own superiority, making it difficult for him to relate to others at all.

As a young married couple Bob and Kathy have learned how to relate. When he comes home from work he rushes down to the basement where she is working. She hears him coming and rushes up to greet him. They meet halfway up the steps and embrace. Jim and Lyn, on the other hand, have been married five years and are frequently defensive toward each other. He returns home in the afternoon expecting her to run up from the basement to meet him. She continues to work expecting him to come down to see her. Jim is sure he has made enough noise for her to hear him, so he refuses to go down. Lyn is certain he knows where she must be, so she refuses to go up. Then they begin playing a little game with each other called "Sitting it Out." Each one knows the other is playing the game, but each pretends he himself is not playing and attempts to keep the other from knowing.

The Structure of Human Relationships

The pendulum swings. In some periods of recent history the accepted standard of value has been the acquiring of knowledge. At other times the development of character has been considered the greatest worth. In certain societies the most important thing in life is a person's class level based either on pedigree or wealth. Each emphasis has been an attempt to reduce the varied values of life by a common denominator.

If one overshadowing criterion for real value can be found in our pluralistic, diversified society today, it is that of relationships. Our university students to their own credit are thinking less about wealth in our materialistic culture and more about relationships. Even their greatest source of thrill-kicks and pleasure-spins are thought of as coming more from relationships and less from purely sensual experience. This explains why the campus prostitute has been put out of business while premarital sex has not necessarily decreased.

An unfortunate phrase that is often heard among students today is "unstructured relationships." There has been a rebellion against structures which are thought to restrict and impair what would otherwise be meaningful relationships. Relationships without structures, without guidelines, without boundaries, without direction are expected by some to produce utopia and resolve all the difficulties of the world.

It is pretty obvious, however, even to the casual observer, that there can be no such thing as an unstructured relationship. A relationship can be well structured or poorly structured, strongly structured or weakly structured, it can be overstructured or barely structured, but it cannot be unstructured. When a relationship becomes unstructured it comes apart. It disintegrates and ceases to exist. Without some structure there is no such thing as a relationship.

While value and consequent happiness are determined by relationships, the quality of relationships is determined by the kind of structure. Correctly structured relationships make possible the greatest happiness, and inappropriately structured relationships create a vulnerability to the most excruciating kind of hurt known to man.

Transactional Analysis deals with one's relationships, or "transactions," with his fellow man. Basic to this system is that the way a person structures his relationships with others is pretty accurately predictable by the personality structures within which he relates to himself. This is often referred to as "structural analysis." Your action toward the other person is not determined by the other's action toward you, but by your own reaction to the other person's action toward you.

What makes a human being react as he does? Why is Irene McIntosh uptight and defensive while Joseph Crenshaw is relaxed and confident? Why does Johnny scream when his mother asks him to pick up his socks, while his sister Mary just ignores her mother's words completely? It is because of the way they operate within, the way they tick on the inside, the way each relates to himself. Unknown to her acquaintances, Irene McIntosh really wanted to relate meaningfully with others, but she was not equipped in her own personality to do so. Joseph Crenshaw would relate to anyone because he related so easily and beautifully with himself. Socrates prayed, "I pray thee, O God, that I may be beautiful within."

It has been recognized for many centuries that there is some kind of internal give-and-take between the differing components of the human personality. The various parts of one's nature are not always in harmony, and there is the conflict of a civil war that ties the personality up in knots. Somewhere inside there is an antagonist, a villain, a vexing blackguard that specializes in causing trouble. This worrisome rogue torments and tantalizes, and sabotages one's best intentions. The apostle Paul said, "When I want to do right, evil lies close at hand" (Rom. 7:21).

Coleridge, the nineteenth-century English writer, spoke of "a dark cold speck at the heart . . . something that must be kept *out of sight* . . . , some secret lodger, whom [one] can neither resolve to reject nor retain."[1] Socrates saw this saboteur as ignorant reason, Plato thought of it as animal nature and Aristotle considered it the perverted human will.

Unpacking Human Personality

The problem is to know how to unpack the human personality. Some have divided it into a lower nature and a higher, or between one's worse self and his better self. Paul spoke of the "old man" and the "new man" (Eph. 4:22, 24, AV). In his *Republic* Plato divided human nature into three elements—the rational, the spirited and the appetitive. Some psychologists have categorized man into conscious mind and unconscious, while others see him as conscious mind, subconscious, semiconscious and unconscious mind. Freud saw every person as consisting of Ego, Id and Superego.

The point is not to attempt to find the *correct* categories, for all of them may be correct from certain perspectives. The point is to define categories that are functional in practical life and understandable to an ordinary person. The categories described by Harris in Transactional Analysis are not new categories, but they have new definitions. Each of the three "persons" within a person—Parent, Child and Adult (spelled with capitals to distinguish them as the "persons" within)—is a certain body of "recordings" from childhood that is preserved in the subconscious memory. These sets of recordings consist of event-data plus data of the feelings that are associated with the event. When the set of recorded Child-data is played back, the Child comes on as the dominant "person" within the person. The Child-feelings erupt as the predominant characteristic of the personality. This eruption of the Parent, Child or Adult is simply a behavioral expression of the "person" within—an expression of either Parent, Child or Adult in what a person says or the way he acts or feels.

These categories roughly parallel traditional categories—the Parent is the moral nature, or culturally conditioned nature, the Child is the emotional nature and the Adult is the rational nature. Or perhaps more accurately, the Parent represents *opinions*, the Child *desires* and the Adult *reason*, or reflection. These parallels I have drawn between Harris' categories and traditional ones are only broadly accurate, but they will serve to help understand the terminology. One principal difference between the two is that traditionally we have thought these three areas were created by God as parts of the human personality with a capacity for content from event- and feeling-data, while Harris thinks of them exclusively as the bundles of impressions or the bodies of recordings received from the environment by the infant. This difference is important in formulating a theology of OKness as we shall see later on. However, Harris makes clear that these categories are used simply as a "sorting device"[2] or as "an easy-to-understand system."[3]

When we speak of Parent, Child and Adult, we are not speaking of three real "persons" within a person, but "three parts of a person."[4] They are psychological states that are easily produced by the bundles of impressions recorded subconsciously in the memory. Speaking of these parts as "persons" becomes a tool to help us see and understand ourselves objectively. It helps us stand outside ourselves and trace our actions and feelings to their inner sources. But it was never intended to enable us to pass the buck on an inner person to take the rap for our errant behavior. Transactional Analysis is intended to discover causes of distorted relationships, to pinpoint reasons for certain behavior. But because the reasons are a part of the person himself, no excuses are passed out. Built into the system is an Adult remedy for the behavioral problems in the Child and Parent, so that the normal person is not exempt from personal responsibility.

Chocolate Cake: Yes or No?

Because the Parent, Child and Adult are characterized by bundles of different kinds of feelings and recorded impressions, it is inevitable that there will be conflict between the persons within. Each reacts in a different way to life situations.

Suppose you have been trying to avoid chocolates to improve your complexion and to stay off sweets in order to reapportion your dimensions. You have finished your meal in a restaurant and the waitress suggests a piece of chocolate fudge cake. If your Child is dominant at the moment, your strongest feeling is for the cake. If your Parent comes on strongest, you have strong feelings of rebuke and prohibitions about the cake. But if your Adult is dominant, your response becomes, "Let's decide this on the basis of my prior commitments and goals, and not worry either about my desires or prohibitions."

Suppose both your Parent and Child come on strong at the moment, and your Adult is not able to dominate. There is tension within yourself, and you become enslaved by the anxiety of indecision. Your mind becomes a pressure cooker and your stomach ties up in knots.

Then you are in no condition to confront a life situation that requires a transaction with another person; you are not able to relate adequately with your neighbor. The telephone rings at the wrong time and you are too tense to communicate easily with your best friend. The conflict that develops in the conversation is a reflection of the conflict already in your mind. The failure to relate to others is caused by your inability to relate adequately to yourself.

Let's look at it another way. The Parent dictates to the Child, "No chocolate cake." The Child retorts to the Parent, "Yes, but I want chocolate cake." The Parent says, "You're just a Child." To which the Child reacts, "Well, then I'll act like a Child." By the time the Adult gets involved in the rivalry, the duel is too heated to restrain. The Adult simply becomes an added source of conflict, attempting to seize control from the belligerent Parent and Child.

This antipathy becomes a pattern of the internal relationships. Feuding begets more feuding. When your life situation requires a relationship with another person, the "persons" within you, accustomed as they are to relating antagonistically one to the other, react antagonistically to the other person.

External relationships with one's fellow man are inevitably characterized by the kind of internal relationships a person has with himself. The response-reaction pattern is the same. The ease and freedom with which Joseph Crenshaw relates to others is a reflection of the way he relates to himself. Interpersonal relationships are meaningful for those who relate to themselves meaningfully. Irene McIntosh's inner conflict expresses itself in outer conflict. Defensiveness toward one's neighbor is a symptom of a lack of peace with oneself. In the New Testament James said, "What is the cause of the fighting and quarrelling that goes on among you? Is it not to be found in the desires which are always at war within you?" (Jas. 4:1).[5]

This is not only true in relationships of peace and conflict. All kinds of human relationships are reflections of similar relationships within the personality. A person who cannot trust himself never has much faith in his fellow man. The woman who suspects what is being said about her is usually the one who is first to gossip about another. The man who expects the worst from the youth of today is usually the one who has gotten a shoddy deal from himself. The person who can take criticism from others is the one who knows how to handle rebuke from his own Parent. The one who hates others deeply inside hates himself, and the one who loves and respects others is the one who loves and respects himself. When Jesus said, "Love thy neighbor as thyself," he was not only giving a commandment. He was also stating a principle that a person does in fact think of his neighbor in the same thought pattern in which he thinks of himself.

If only the personality could be integrated! If the Parent and Child could be harmonized with the Adult under one head, tuned to the same wave length and turned to the same channel! We can never expect our social transactions to be smooth and pleasant until the variant components of our personalities are playing in the same key and directed by the same Conductor.

The question that follows is this: How can a person relate meaningfully to himself? How can the inner conflict cease? How can one's Parent and Child be harmonized with the Adult? Is there a psychological state available that can accommodate the needs of each personality component? This we shall see in the following chapters.

2

RELATING TO GOD

*O*n New Year's Day of 1974 Charles M. Schulz, the sagacious creator of the *Peanuts* comic strip, was featured as Grand Marshall of the Tournament of Roses parade in Pasadena. In his strip for that day, Linus finds Lucy watching the parade on television and asks, "Has the Grand Marshall gone by yet?" Lucy replies, "Yeah, you missed him. . . . But he wasn't anyone you ever heard of!"

The obvious point is that Schulz' own created characters were not aware of their own creator. How like man and his Creator!

The Creator and His Creatures
Our Creator is eminently before us and we often fail to recognize his presence. We see the active works of God all around us and we attribute them to other sources. We use the brains God has given us and we rearrange what he has created into machines, industrial plants, modern homes

and spacecraft, and then we think we are the creators. We are like the gnat that alighted on a wagon as it was being pulled by a team of mules up a dusty country road. The gnat looked behind him and exclaimed, "My, what a dust I'm raising!"

Yet only a minority of mankind has been totally unaware of a Creator. We discover in man of all cultures throughout recorded history both a burning desire and an irrepressible belief that he can in some way relate to the Source of his existence.

Regardless of the way he may have created the universe, the conviction that God is ultimate Creator is a presupposition that need not be argued here. Christians hold that God has created man with a capacity to understand and feel his position in the universe as a created individual rather than creator, and that thus men belong to an order of created things. In our society we have luxuries, commodities of convenience, machines to do our work, television to provide our entertainment, even computers to do our thinking. It is not surprising that we get a feeling of self-sufficiency and forget that our existence is derived. Inevitably, however, these little gods fail us because they are not big enough to be our gods, and we are driven back in desperation to the meaninglessness, the emptiness, the inadequacy of our lives without God. Being created rather than creator, man within himself is never sufficient for himself. Standing alone he is forever not-OK.

There are some central issues of life that are common to most major religions of the world. While they have their crucial differences at important points, most agree that something is dreadfully wrong with man and that the "something wrong" can be explained in terms of his estrangement from God. Built into each of these religious systems in its own peculiar way is the notion that a relationship with God will meet man's deepest need and solve his greatest problem—and this presupposes man's capacity for such a relationship. The differences that separate the religions have to do with how this God-man relationship can be established, and these differences are critical, but belief in the creature's capacity to relate to the ultimate is common to all.

Augustine in *The City of God* expressed the common feeling of man in every age, "O Lord. Thou hast made us for Thyself, and we are restless until we find our rest in Thee." The New Testament teaches that man has been built with a capacity for divine occupancy. Paul said, "You are God's temple" (1 Cor. 3:16). Man is so constructed mentally and emotionally that he can entertain the divine Presence, and he has the psychological structures for relating meaningfully with the God-personality. This is the reason it is impossible to explain *away* a relationship with God merely by *explaining* it psychologically.

A Meaning for Man

It is interesting that animals seem to look down—to sex, sustenance and survival—and they are satisfied. But man looks down to sex, sustenance and survival, and he keeps becoming disillusioned and is never satisfied. He gets the feeling that he is going in the wrong direction on a one-way street. Somehow man keeps looking upward, standing on tiptoe, reaching for beauty, for the ultimate, for God.

In a recent *Peanuts* strip, Schulz has Snoopy on his doghouse sighing, "Everything seems empty. . . . I search the skies, but I can find no meaning! No meaning!" Suddenly Charlie Brown appears with a dish of dog food, and Snoopy leaps up and shouts, "Ah! Meaning!"

The universal experience of man, however, is that he cannot be so easily satisfied in his search for meaning and reality. He has an insatiable hunger for something beyond what satisfies his physical hunger, and without this true meaning he feels estranged from himself and from the universe. He feels anchorless, detached from reality, directionless. He begins to believe that his planet is a cosmic orphanage in a crazy, mixed-up universe that offers no pattern for real living and no direction for meaningful destiny. Yet he keeps searching, always hoping to stumble upon a chance encounter with a Personality who can integrate all of life's parts into one harmonious whole.

At this point the inquisitive person may ask where the capacity to relate to God originated. Did God create man originally with this capacity? Has it developed through evolutionary processes through millennia of history? Is it a mere happenstance resulting from subconscious recordings of event-data and feeling-data which we classify into Parent, Child and Adult? If this should be the case, it must be asked where the infant got the capacity to receive and store such data, for the fact *that* he stores this data does not in any way explain *why* he does so. If this should be explained by the physiochemical activity of brain cells, the question still remains why the brain can store such data chemically when the foot cannot and where the brain acquired such a capacity to function chemically in this way.

A recent turn of events has found the long established

Darwinian hypothesis being called into serious question by reputable philosophers of science. In 1971 a paper was read before the annual meeting of the American Association for the Advancement of Science by John Moore, a professor of natural science at Michigan State, charging that evolution has become a "religion" rather than a science and that scientific experimentation fails to confirm what would be expected from a strict Darwinism. B. P. Dotsenko, a former top nuclear scientist for the Soviet Union who defected to the West and now teaches at Waterloo Lutheran University in Ontario, recently said,

> One of the most fundamental laws of nature that interested me was the law of entropy, concerning the most probable behavior of particles (molecules, atoms, electrons, etc.) of any physical system. This law, put simply, states that if any system is given to itself it will decay very quickly, inasmuch as particles composing any system have a tendency to run wild. It means that all the material world should have turned into a cloud of chaotic dust a long, long time ago. . . . It dawned upon me that the world is being held in existence by a nonmaterial power that is capable of overruling this destructive entropy.[1]

Even Alfred North Whitehead, the twentieth-century popularizer of process philosophy in America, wrote:

> Life itself is comparatively deficient in survival value. . . . Only inorganic things persist for great lengths of time. . . . The problem set by the doctrine of evolution is to explain how complex organisms with such deficient survival power ever evolved. . . . If we survey the universe of nature, mere static survival seems to be the

general rule, accompanied by a slow decay. . . . a slow slipping away. . . .[2]

At best organic evolution can only explain *what* happened, and *how* it happened that a unicellular organism emerged in primeval slime, but it cannot begin to explain *why* the amorphous blob ever became a living organism. Even less can it explain why man of all animals has a capacity to relate to God! Some kind of intentional divine creative action within whatever evolutionary process may have been at work is required for an explanation of man's capacity for God. The biblical account of man's origin reads, "The LORD . . . breathed into his nostrils the breath of life; and man became a living being" (Gen. 2:7).

God and PAC

Some theologians have questioned whether Harris' categories of Parent, Child and Adult are adequate for an understanding of man's creatureliness and the way he is able to relate to his Creator. Personally, I think they are adequate if we understand that these categories are only intended to explain man's action and reaction, and not the totality of man's spiritual nature. If they are to be used to explain the creature-Creator relationship, however, the categories must be expanded to include the divinely created capacity for God. This means there is an element in man's ego-state categories that has not come from data recordings —an element given directly by the Creator to man. This capacity for God is a distinctively religious claim which the behavioral scientist cannot make without getting out of his field. If we allow the categories of Parent, Child and Adult to be broad enough to include this created God-capacity, then we find in these categories the tools for understanding something of man's sense of isolation without God as well as something of his capacity to interact with the God-personality.

This capacity to relate to the creative Source of life has often been spoken of in spacial terms. It has been referred to as a bottomless pit in the soul or as a vacuum in the personality waiting to be filled with God, or as a God-shaped blank. Of course, these spacial metaphors can be useful in understanding what it means to have a capacity for God. Indeed, the Bible itself speaks of being "filled" with the Holy Spirit.

In order to use the categories of Parent, Child and Adult, however, this capacity to relate to God has to be understood in functional terms. The capacity for God, then, seems to be distributed among all three categories of the human personality rather than being a separate category in itself.

This is to say that the Parent, Child and Adult each has its own functional role in relating to God. Each of the three depends on a proper relationship with God in order to function in harmony with the other two and to produce a balanced, integrated personality. Without this relationship with the Creator, each "person" within the person has its own peculiar problems and is incapable of relating harmoniously with the other two.

We shall now look into both the need for God and the capacity to relate to God in Child, Parent and Adult in order to see how this God-man relationship can produce the needed harmony between the three personality "persons."

3

OKNESS FOR THE CHILD

"*W*hat a piece of work is man! how noble in reason! how infinite in faculty! in form and moving how express and admirable! in action how like an angel! in apprehension how like a god!"[1] This celebration of man by Shakespeare's Hamlet enunciates something of the near inexhaustible mystery of man. When one begins to realize that man has both the need and the capacity for the personality of God, it staggers the imagination.

It is important to remember that a person is *one* person in spite of the three "persons" within him. Though one or another of the inside "persons" may come on stronger at any given time, the Parent, Child and Adult all converge into one person—which may be called *ego, personality center* or *conscious awareness.* While each of the inward "persons" has its own need for God, it is the total person that relates to God. When my Child needs the love and security of God, it is *I* that needs that love and security. And when my Adult needs the assurance of purpose and direction, it is *I* that needs it.

Two of a person's basic needs can only be fully met by a relationship with God. One is to discover the *reason* for my existence, and this belongs to the Adult. The other is to experience *security* in my existence, and this belongs to the Child. These two primary needs are so inextricably related that neither can be fulfilled alone. Each of the two gives rise to the other, and neither can be met until the other is met. The dilemma is solved when the person as a whole has an established relationship with God.

The Child Becomes Not-OK

Man's need to discover his reason for existence is a result of his capacity to relate to God. While an animal has a mind, it probably does not have a rational mind. Man seems to be the only creature on earth that is able to ask what kind of creature he is. And he seems to be the only one who can ask questions about the ultimate reason for existence. An answer only in the spacial-temporal or physical-social contexts is not satisfactory because man belongs to a higher context. He is never satisfied with the closed system of physical causes, and he is ever trying to break out into a larger dimension.

The failure of the Adult to discover this ultimate reason for existence produces the feeling of insecurity in the Child. We say the Child becomes not-OK. Without the direction and guidelines that should come from an understanding of one's reason for existence, the Adult is not equipped to guide the feelings of the Child. Consequently, the Child feels estranged from true purpose, detached from reality, short-circuited from God. He sometimes feels like a stranger to himself, and he begins to wonder whether he is an authentic person after all. The Adult has discovered no ultimate design and destiny in life, and the Child therefore has anxieties about life and uncertainties about death.

While there may be times that we feel not-OK when we really are OK, there cannot be a sustained *feeling* of OKness until we are in a position of *being* OK.

The book of Genesis first pictures the man God made as feeling "at home" with God. He was OK. But something happened that destroyed man's relationship with God, and he became estranged from God. Having made himself the center of the universe, man finds himself a stranger in the universe. He has no emotional nest in the world because he has no security pocket in the universe. He is out of his natural habitat, for he was created for God. Without God, he is hopelessly plagued with homelessness.

Friedrich Nietzsche, the German philosopher-poet who first popularized the phrase, "God is dead," has been quoted as saying, "Alone I confront a tremendous problem. It is a forest in which I lose myself, a virgin forest. I need help. . . . I need a master. . . . But I find no one. . . . I am alone."[2] It was this existential dilemma that drove Nietzsche to a position of nihilism after he rejected God. Nihilism is the philosophy of ultimate not-OKness, and it seems to be finally the only alternative philosophically for the person who has no relationship with God. For the person who was built for God and is yet isolated from the God for whom he was made, the world system is all wrapped up in nothingness.

The tragic death of the wife of a foreign ambassador to

the United Nations was attributed to her desperate loneliness in the middle of a city of nine million persons. Upon coming to New York she had been presented a booklet by the city which said, "Take advantage of the friendliness of New Yorkers." But she was driven by an uncontrollable sense of loneliness to push her two babies and herself from the window of her eighteenth-floor Manhattan apartment. Companionship with friends and neighbors will dispel human loneliness, but it can never drive away existential loneliness. A person's Child may feel OK in the world, but it has an underlying not-OKness in the universe that cannot be made OK by human relationships. Relationships in the world may get one's mind off the need for companionship with God, but the need can only be satisfied by God himself.

It was this existential estrangement that brought Svetlana Stalin to the United States seeking a new life. The daughter of the late Soviet dictator said simply, "I found it was impossible to exist without God in one's heart." The Child may feel OK in society by proper adjustment within his social contacts. But man was made ultimately for a higher social order, a bigger world than this, and the Child remains deeply not-OK in the universe until it becomes OK with God.

Crisis of Identity

When we talk about the reason for existence, there are two sides of the coin that pose problems for the Adult. The two sides are enunciated in philosophy by distinguishing between the "efficient cause" and the "final cause." We can think of the one as *what* caused my existence and the other as *why* my existence was caused. Often we use the word *reason* in both ways. I might say, "The reason I exist is that God caused me." Or I might say, "The reason God caused me was that he had a purpose for me." For the sake of clarity, we will think of *reason* in the first sense as *cause* and in the second sense as *purpose*.

Now when I discover the reason for my existence in both senses, two of the greatest problems facing me as a modern man are immediately resolved for my Adult. The first has been called the *crisis of identity*. Modern man is asking, What *caused* me? Who am I? A college student wrote, "We [younger people] are the hope of the world, but we have no hope. We only have hope in ourselves, and who are we? We cannot even discover" who we are.[3] Through a relationship with my Creator, I discover who I am—I am the created of God, *I am a child of God*. This tells me who I am in the universe.

With this information, my Adult is equipped to deal with the not-OK feelings of estrangement in my Child. There may be times when I still will feel a human loneliness, but I need never again feel existential loneliness. Realizing who I am, I no longer feel like a cosmic orphan floating in space. I have a home base in the universe. I have something to latch onto when everything else gives way. I feel the security of *belonging*—belonging to God, to the ultimate, to everything, when there is nothing else worth belonging to. I feel plugged into the source of everything. I have access to the nerve center of eternity. Because I am a child of God, the crisis of identity has been resolved. Ultimately, deeply and essentially, my Child is OK. My Adult can now turn off my Child's not-OK-in-the-world recordings and turn on the newer OK-with-God recordings.

Crisis in Meaning

The other problem—the flip side of the reason for my existence—has been called the *crisis in meaning*. Modern man is not only asking, Who am I? He is also asking, Why am I? What is the *purpose* for my existence? When I have an established relationship with my Creator, I discover that if I am created by God I am created for his purpose. I begin to realize that I can find my true fulfillment in him. My Adult is now equipped to deal with my Child's feelings of uselessness, worthlessness and purposelessness. My life has new meaning.

Because man was created for a purpose, he cannot live without a purpose. If he loses his real purpose for existence by losing his relationship with God, he will invent a false purpose that may center in wealth, or pleasure or social status. But these purposes do not square with reality because they are not the purposes for which he was made. Life becomes a constant battle for adjustment and a perpetual accommodation instead of true fulfillment.

In September of 1973 Ed "Buzz" Aldrin, the second earthling ever to set foot on the lunar surface, was featured in an interview on NBC's Today Show. He discussed his emotional break that followed his moon mission and his gradual recovery. The consuming passion of his life, he explained, had been to get to the moon. For many years he worked tirelessly before finally achieving his goal. Once the goal had been attained there was no higher goal, he said, and he became disillusioned. In his autobiography, *Return to Earth*, Aldrin says, "Without a goal I was like an inert ping-pong ball being batted about by the whims and motivations of others." The result was serious emotional disturbance.

Man was made for a higher purpose and a greater goal than reaching the moon. No lesser goal than God, no smaller purpose than the purposes of God, can give man's spirit true meaning and lasting fulfillment. The Child remains tormented with not-OKness until the Adult discovers the ultimate purpose in life.

Marilyn Monroe once confessed when she was at the height of her popularity and glamor, "I feel as though it's all happening to someone right next to me. I'm close—I can feel it, I can hear it, but it isn't really me."[4] The tragedy of modern man is that he thinks the reason for his existence is in himself, and then he wonders why he has frustration rather than fulfillment.

When the Adult understands that his true purpose for living is in God who created him, the Child is able to feel new meaning, purpose and direction in life. A cohesive ingredient seems to run through life's distorted and confused puzzle, pulling up the loose ends and centering everything on something ultimate. The disconcerting things of life are now seen from a new perspective. The Adult sees a divine design in life, and the Child feels a Supernatural Hand directing his destiny. The person gets the feeling that he is now cooperating with the purpose for which he was born. The Child feels OKness in usefulness, worthwhileness and meaning.

So when my relationship with God is completed and intact, my Adult understands first the *cause* of my existence and therefore *who* I am. From this my Child feels the OK security of *belonging*, and the *crisis in identity* has been resolved. Second, from my relationship with God my Adult understands the *purpose* of my existence and therefore *why*

I am. From this my Child feels the OK security of importance, direction and destiny, and the *crisis in meaning* has been resolved.

Adult and Child: Reason and Experience

I have said that the failure of the Adult to discover the ultimate reason (the cause and the purpose) for existence produces in the Child the sense of not-OKness both in estrangement and meaninglessness. Now I wish to turn the record over and say that the estrangement in the Child often accounts for the Adult's inability to discover the reason for existence.

The point is that the relationship with God is established neither with the Adult nor with the Child, but with the person as a whole person which includes both the Adult and the Child. The relationship includes both an Adult recognition and affirmation of the relationship plus a Child experience of the relationship.

The need for belonging properly belongs to the Child. It includes the desire for personality intimacy and a spiritual oneness, the longing to belong to an adequate relationship. When one has a meaningful encounter with God, it is the Child that experiences that relationship. A relationship is not something to be thought—it is something to be experienced. It can be thought about by the Adult, recognized and confirmed, but a relationship by definition is something to be experienced. And the experiencing is the function of the Child.

Now the Adult does not have sufficient data to discover the reason for one's existence without the help of the Child's experience of God. By reflection, contemplation and study, the Adult may come a long way toward understanding the reason for existence, but it is finally dependent on additional data that can only be supplied by the Child's experience of God. The Adult can never understand fully the reason for existence until the reason is discovered in a relationship with God, and that relationship is experienced by the Child. This is why Karl Barth has emphasized what he calls "given faith" and has strongly denied the mind's ability to lead one rationally to God.

The Adult may rationally understand what a relationship with God is and may affirm such a relationship, but the Adult affirmation alone is not a relationship. It takes the Child's experience of the relationship in order for the relationship to exist. And it is from this relationship experienced by the Child that the Adult discovers the reason for existence. This is why one's relationship with God is often called an "existential experience."

When I say, however, that the Adult depends on the Child's experience to give the Adult knowledge of the God-relationship, I am not implying that the Adult cannot have knowledge of the relationship. To say that a person cannot be led rationally all the way to God without the experience is not to say that the relationship is irrational.

This is where a large number of existentialists from Kierkegaard to Barth have made their mistake. While the Christian cannot rely on intellectual reasoning *alone* to lead him into the God-relationship, he does depend upon a rational Adult recognition of truth and correctness of ideas to distinguish a truly Christian experience from a mere neurotic or ecstatic experience and to define an intelligent basis for faith as different from Kierkegaard's "blind leap" or

Barth's "irrational faith." Even though we depend on what Barth called "given faith" (that is, God's revelation of himself to man), what one may think of as "given faith" is subject to the scrutiny of the Adult mind to distinguish it from superstition.

Without an adequate understanding in the Adult of who God is, what he is like and what he requires, the chances of an adequate experiential relationship with God are slim. The average person will get lost in the woods unless he has a map or a compass. The person who says, "I don't care about theology, I just want to experience God" is really saying, "I don't want my Child to be directed by my Adult." Without Adult guidelines the Child becomes vulnerable to all kinds of mystical experiences. Sooner or later the person goes off the deep end, and the mysticism is like quicksand— soft, smooth and mushy, with no resistance. It may be the easiest way to go, but there is no solidness to stand on, no anchor for support, and the person is soon swallowed up.

There are many of us who are convinced that we have discovered with our Adult minds reasonable and adequate guidelines for faith and Christian experience in the Judeo-Christian Scriptures. When the Child's experience of God is structured by the principles expressed in the Bible, a relationship with God is possible which is true to reality and meets the highest Adult need to discover the meaning of existence and the deepest emotional need of the Child for security in that existence.

In this chapter we have seen something of the interdependence of the Child and Adult. An Adult reason for existence is required for a Child sense of security. A Child experience of a relationship with God is necessary for an

Adult reason for existence. And an Adult understanding of the character of God and the nature of the God-relationship is important as a guideline for the Child experience. In the following chapter I want us to observe where we get our concept of God and how we can have a concept of God true to what God really is.

4

WHAT KIND OF GOD IS GOD?

*H*ave you ever seriously tried to relate meaningfully to an odious, demanding personality who would not move an inch in your direction? Then you know how difficult it is to relate to a God who is totally indifferent to the needs and desires of man.

Or again, have you ever felt smothered by an overly eager would-be friend who is mawkish and sticky as he reaches out to you? Just so unappealing and impossible is one's relationship to a soft and supersentimental God.

One of the greatest obstacles to a meaningful relationship with God is a false concept of what God is like, a concept that has emerged from recordings in the Child and Parent rather than an Adult examination of the available evidence.

Without an objective scriptural guideline for our Adult faith, the concept of God for most of us comes simply from our Child and Parent recordings of feeling-data. For those rare persons who have a superb quality of feeling recordings, their concept of God may approximate the biblical picture of God. For average persons with poorer quality recordings, the image of God is warped and distorted unless the Adult has fashioned the God-concept by objective guidelines.

Ordinarily the person whose parents were permissive and indulgent toward him when he was small gets an image of God as soft, sentimental and characterless. For the one whose parents were harsh, strict and demanding, God has an image of a tyrant. The first arises from recordings in the Child and the second from those in the Parent. Persons so fortunate as to have had parents who commanded in them both a respect for their authority and a response to their love usually arrive quite easily at a biblical concept of God as both sovereign Lord and beneficent Father.

God as State Trooper

The Child and Parent, however, continue to record feelings beyond the years of infancy, so the concept of God may be constantly changing to coincide with the latest body of recorded feeling-data. Six-year-old Sarah is disappointed when Santa Claus does not bring her what she had expected, and she shifts the new image of Santa to God, and then understands him as undependable, sponsoring flashy commercials with faulty products and failing to deliver on his promises. At age twelve she detects inconsistencies in the lives of local church leaders whom she has identified as representatives of God, so God is thought of as phony.

At eighteen she feels threatened by the demands of the Christian faith on her lifestyle, so she considers God as an antagonist, an opponent, an enemy to be opposed. Later on she contemplates the suffering and evil in the world and begins to think of God as brutal and barbaric. Underneath all the new recordings, there has been through the years a feeling of guilt, and from this God has been understood all along as a state trooper with a billy club in hand, or as a cosmic combination of prosecuting attorney, prejudiced jury and relentless judge all in one person.

It is impossible to have a meaningful relationship with this kind of God.

God as a Good Old Boy

Six-year-old David, on the other hand, learns that all he has to do is announce to his parents what he wants for Christmas and Santa lavishes upon him in great abundance every plaything he has requested. David soon gets the idea that he is the center of the world and God is obligated to respond to every whim and fancy. His requests become demands to which he thinks God is forced to comply. The God-concept that evolves is that of a gutless, spineless Father Christmas sitting in a back seat in the universe passing out sticks of candy to win the favor of man.

At fourteen David joins the church, and the local folk make such a fuss over him that he begins to feel he has done God a special honor and that God should feel congratulated that he now has such a fine young man on deck. He gets the notion he can go through life placating God with an occasional nod to keep him off his back so that he can continue selfishly to be the center of his own little world. Before long God is considered little more than a squalling brat who threatens to mess up your playhouse unless you keep a pacifier in his mouth.

In high school David stars as an athlete. He has brains and talent and personality. Day after day he sees the public bowing before his plays on the football field, or his talent on the debate team or his excellence in classwork. He feels the love and support and appreciation of those around him. The concept of God begins to emerge as number one member of his fan club, the leader of the cheering section, with a special seat in the grandstand for leading the applause.

Sooner or later God's image evolves into a good old boy, a back slapper, one who enjoys being taken advantage of. His love is available to be used as a tool to achieve one's selfish ends, as a crowbar to pry loose difficult situations or as a shock absorber to cushion the road surface of life. He is devoid of holiness and justice, and his love is so soft and profuse that he winks at the sins of his creatures. God becomes a pushover, a gullible sucker who can easily be taken for all he is worth.

It should go without being said that a meaningful relationship with this kind of God is also impossible.

The Real Mr. God

The question is, What is God really like? A little girl wrote a letter to God and said, in the words of a popular television show, "Will the real Mr. God please stand up?" How can we discover the real Mr. God?

When I was a child I received quite a number of spankings from both my mom and my dad. Before each spanking, time was taken to explain to me why the punishment was being administered, and I can never recall having received a lick from either parent out of anger or as an on-thespot reaction to something I had done. I was taught the principles of justice and retribution involved in punishment, and I was shown the change in my behavior that was expected from the punishment. I learned there was always a higher authority to which I was responsible.

Both parents had told me that it hurt them to apply the spanking as badly as it hurt me to receive it. This was difficult to believe until once after a paddling from my father I turned around to see his eyes filled with tears. This experience fixed in my mind what I had felt at even a much earlier age—that my parents were authority, but that the authority was exercised with love. Many times my Child felt the not-OKness of disapproval, but never once has my Child felt not-OK in their affection. It was their love and understanding that kept me disarmed and created within me an ability to accept the authority without seriously reacting. This responsibility to authority enabled me later on to accept civil authority without being belligerent and to accept my responsibility to God without being defensive. I was fortunate enough to feel from the data supplied by my parents that God was neither a pushover nor a tyrant, that I was responsible to his authority and also the recipient of his love.

Now all three of these concepts of God that I have described—God as tyrant, God as sentimental pushover and God as authority-love—arise primarily from recordings in the Child and Parent. The concept of God emerges first as a feeling in the Child or a restrictiveness in the Parent, and then it evolves into a concept that can be examined by the Adult. It is my conviction that the average person goes through life with the concept of God acquired from his Child or Parent and rarely exposes this concept to the scrutiny of his Adult. If the concept is that of a tyrant or a push-over, it is improbable that he will ever have a meaningful relationship with God until the concept is changed.

The task of the Adult, however, is not quite so simple as gaining a concept of God that will accommodate a meaningful relationship with man. Primarily the Adult must discover a *true* concept of God that resembles what God really is, whether or not that concept will allow for a meaningful God-man relationship.

God's Gracious Self-Disclosure

At first it seems rather presumptuous to assume that the Adult may be able to arrive at a correct concept of God. Richard Hooker wrote in the sixteenth century, "Our soundest knowledge is to know that we know him not as indeed he is. . . . Our safest eloquence is our silence, when we confess without confession that his glory is inexplicable, his greatness above our capacity and reach."[1] Certainly it seems arrogant to expect the Adult, from its obscure position in the universe and with its finite limitations, to discover the nature of the infinite God. The apostle Paul exclaimed, "The world did not know God through wisdom" (1 Cor. 1:21).

The claim to know what God is like is the haughtiest, most conceited claim ever made—*unless* God has placed himself within the Adult's field of discovery. If God has revealed himself on the level of man's understanding as the Christian Scriptures claim, it follows that the Adult is in a position to recognize the fact of this divine self-disclosure. If the fact of God's revelation can be accepted by the reasonable Adult, then the content of the revelation—what God is like—can be affirmed by the Adult though it may not be rationally understood. The Adult can affirm a concept of God which it may not understand *if* it has intelligently affirmed the fact of the revelation which contains the concept of God.

That such a revelation will withstand rational scrutiny is an argument that does not properly belong to this book. But there are many of us who are convinced with our Adult minds, though with great awe and humility, that God has disclosed what he is like both in the Scriptures and in Jesus whom the Scriptures depict.

Certainly we can never know *all* of God any more than we can comprehend all the ocean by observing a goblet full of ocean. Nevertheless, even a goblet of ocean reveals the quality of ocean water.

The interesting point is that the Adult concept of God which is drawn from this revelation will accommodate a God-man relationship, for it is identical with the authority-love concept held by the person with the superb quality of recordings. Throughout the Bible we see God as sovereign ruler of the universe, the absolute ultimate authority to which every man is ultimately responsible. But we also see God throughout both the Old Testament and the New as a God of love, kindness, patience and forgiveness.

Similarly in the teachings of Jesus, God's "in person" revelation, we hear the voice of authority over and again: "Verily I say unto you. . . ." But we also see his tender concern for humanity, his love for the unloved, his forgiveness to the sinner.

Even more than in his teachings, however, we see this kind of God mirrored in his voluntary death at the cross.

When I hear the deep agonizing breath of Calvary's victim and the pleading petition to the Father to forgive the terrorism of his brutal killers, I hear God saying, "I love and I forgive. But can't you see that my forgiveness is not cheap, sentimental or superficial? Look, I am dying for you. My love is tough and stubborn. It is a costly love!"

When I see Jesus on that cross, I do not see God either as a tyrant or as a pushover, but I see in that gutsiest act of history the kind of God I would be willing to give everything to really know. He is the kind of God who commands my highest Adult respect and my deepest Child love, the kind of God my Child longs for, and the kind of God my Adult thinks will change my life—if only I can relate with him.

I can respond to his love because it is strong and courageous rather than soft and sentimental. And I can accept his authority because it is kind and considerate rather than harsh and tyrannical. As C. S. Lewis once said, "The hardness of God is kinder than the softness of men."[2]

In this kind of God which my Adult has discovered in Jesus, I find all that my Child needs—forgiveness when I feel guilty, security when I feel anchorless, challenge when I feel purposeless, comfort when I feel loneliness, a sense of belonging when I feel detached, love when I feel empty. It all fits together—I was made for this kind of God!

Relating with this God provides my Child with an OK-ness that transcends any not-OKness in the world. Over three centuries ago it was expressed by the English writer Francis Quarles:

> In having all things, and not Thee, what have I?
> Not having Thee what have my labors got?
> Let me enjoy but Thee, what further crave I?

And having Thee alone, what have I not?
I wish nor sea nor land; nor would I be
Possess'd of heaven, heaven unpossess'd of Thee.

5

WHERE DOES GUILT COME FROM?

*I*n 1972 an old man bowed with age limped into the sheriff's office in Jacksonville, Florida, to make a confession. Since 1935 he had carried the guilt of a murder he had committed, and he had to get it off his chest. For thirty-seven years he had borne a weight of guilt that had almost ground the life out of his spirit, and now he could carry it no longer.

Nothing on earth is quite so devastating to the human personality as a personal sense of guilt. It impedes creative powers, distracts attention, inhibits concentration, drains off emotional energy, shackles personal efficiency. Often the guilt is simply from some minor offense and is barely recognized. But it filters down into subconsciousness and erupts as fear or hostility. It causes distress, depression and despair, and has driven thousands to suicide.

How can guilt be handled adequately? What can the person do who is pestered and tormented by a nagging, harrowing sense of guilt? The categories of Transactional

Analysis are excellent tools for understanding guilt so that it can be overcome and the human spirit liberated.

I Accuse

In the last few chapters we have discussed the interaction between the Child and Adult, and we have seen that an adequate relationship with God gives the Adult a reason for existence and the Child the OKness of belonging and meaning. The greatest obstruction, however, to a relationship with God is guilt, and to understand this we need to look at the Parent and see how the Parent interacts with the Child and Adult.

The Parent has two functions, best understood by distinguishing between Controlling Parent and Nurturing Parent. The controlling, restricting activity of the Parent produces guilt, and the nurturing, forgiving activity of the Parent eliminates the guilt. In this chapter we are concerned with the controlling, accusing function of the Parent.

The feeling of guilt belongs to the Child, but it is produced in the Child by the Parent. The Parent is the accuser —pointing the finger, furrowing the brow, throwing disdainful and accusing glances with sharply cutting eyes. The Child feels beaten down, self-defeated, at fault, unworthy and guilty.

What is there in the Parent that so enables it to accuse and produce guilt in the Child? In the Controlling Parent we discover at least two active forces which must combine in order for guilt to be produced.

The first I will call *oughtness* for short, and allow it to stand for what is commonly called conscience, the moral principle within or the sense of moral oughtness. In every culture in every age man has recognized an inner sense of oughtness and ought-not-ness, though there is an unlimited number of opinions about *what* one ought and ought not do. Two persons may dispute over *what* is the right thing to do, but the fact of their disagreement shows that they both agree the right thing should be done.

Perhaps this principle of morality comes into sharpest focus when seen in contrast to the desires of the Child. A conflict situation is set up between Parent and Child. When there is no conflict between the two, the moral principle of oughtness is not so easily detected. It is the conflict that exposes the oughtness as a force to be reckoned with.

The Source of Oughtness

Where does this moral sense of oughtness and ought-not-ness have its source? It may be convenient to say that it is culturally conditioned (data recordings), but it is not so easy to be convincing that the sense of oughtness, or should-do-ness, is developed by the incentives of praise and reward. It is only obvious that praise and reward condition a person to act *so as to receive the praise or reward.* It is not obvious that praise and reward condition one to act morally right *simply because it is right.*

Even less can one be convinced that the sense of ought-not-ness comes from having been shamed or made to feel guilty. How could the feelings of shame and guilt ever be produced by the Parent in the Child without the prior sense of should-do and should-not-do already in the Parent? To say the sense of ought-not-ness causes the guilt and being made to feel guilty causes the sense of ought-not-ness is to reason in a circle.

The available evidence points to God as the ultimate source of moral order. At the heart of the consciousness of guilt is the realization of having sinned against God. Jesus told the story of the Prodigal Son who, upon returning to his human father, confessed, "I have sinned against heaven" (Lk. 15:21). After King David had committed the grievous sins of adultery and murder, his guilt drove him to confess to God, "Against thee, thee only, have I sinned, and done that which is evil in thy sight" (Ps. 51:4).

The concept of moral oughtness, which no one can deny, is a farce unless it has its source in the ultimate, in God. Without an absolute as its source, what a person does may be nice or crude, lovely or ugly, sweet or sour, but it cannot be right or wrong. Without the ultimate in the universe to which man is responsible, the notion of right or wrong is empty. *Should* and *should-not*, *ought* and *ought-not* are meaningless terms apart from a God-centered moral order, for they cannot be intelligently explained without reference to God. *What* is considered right or wrong is another matter, but *that* an act is considered right or wrong requires a God to be intelligible.

This moral oughtness in the Parent is a part of man's capacity to relate with God, a capacity whose source is God rather than the recorded data from life. Further, to admit there is a God behind the moral order is to admit that man is responsible to this God and that this God of moral order is the final Judge of man.

Conscience Requires Knowledge
Along with this moral sense of oughtness is a second force

in the Controlling Parent, both of which combine to produce the guilt in the Child. This is what I call the *opinions* of what is right. Oughtness does not give any clue as to *what* is right, but only that there *is* a right and that one *should do* whatever the right may be. The oughtness depends on knowledge of what is right in order to impress the person what to do. The sense of oughtness may be understood as a depository for the Parent data recordings of *what* is right. The opinion of what is right is the content for oughtness, and without it the sense of oughtness would be in limbo.

When Queen Mary rejected what John Knox had suggested, she said, "My conscience says not so." And Knox replied, "Conscience, Madam, requires knowledge."

At the Diet of Worms in 1521 Martin Luther took his courageous stand on the basis of his conscience. But he realized that conscience alone is empty without specific knowledge of what is right, and he said, "My conscience remains captive to the word of God."

It is a combination of the sense of oughtness and the opinions of rightness that produces the not-OKness of guilt in the Child, neither one of which by itself would be capable of producing the guilt. When Johnny tells a fib, his opinion of what is right lets him know that he has done wrong. This could easily be handled without any accompanying feelings of guilt if Johnny did not have the sense of oughtness to tell him he should do what is right and not do what is wrong. But when the sense of oughtness says you should not do whatever is wrong and the opinion of what is right says deception is wrong, Johnny experiences the not-OKness of guilt.

The failure to distinguish between the *that* of oughtness

and the *what* of rightness accounts for the fallacious advice in a hit record several years ago, "Let your conscience be your guide."

Now if the moral oughtness has been created in the Parent by the Creator, where does the Parent get its opinions of what is right? It is generally accepted that this information is ordinarily acquired from one's teaching and cultural conditioning. A person's opinion about what is right reflects the data received from his home, his early training, his community, his school and teachers, his church and pastor. It is a part of the body of recordings from early childhood which he has retained in subconscious memory.

From this it is obvious that a person's idea of what is right may be excellent or it may be the most warped, prejudiced idea any blockhead ever had.Oughtness has no way to distinguish the good opinions of what is right from the lousy, so the conscience will drive a person with twisted opinions just as much as the person with better opinions. There are sincere persons on opposite sides of political, social and theological issues, and each is driven with a strong sense of oughtness. Those on both sides consider it a moral obligation to do what they are convinced is right.

On one occasion Jesus said to his disciples, "The hour is coming when whoever kills you will think he is offering service to God" (Jn. 16:2). Later on Paul explained why he had persecuted Christians prior to his conversion. He said, "I myself was convinced that I ought to do many things in opposing the name of Jesus" (Acts 26:9). Notice, he really *thought* that he *ought*.

I can conceive how Mr. John Doe has the notion that the stricter he is in rearing his children the better it is for them.

They are given no freedom of expression, no leisure time, disciplinary punishment beyond the extent of the offense. They develop emotional problems which are reflected in their interpersonal relationships. It actually hurts Daddy Doe to have to be so demanding, but he thinks he is doing the little Does a great service. To him it becomes a matter of conscience, a moral duty to rear them "properly," and he does so at great sacrifice of his own feelings.

Now when a person does not conform to what he thinks is right, the sense of oughtness combines with his opinion of what is right and produces guilt in the Child—regardless of whether he has a good or poor opinion of what is right. Billy may be taught to fight for his rights, and Harry is taught never to fight at all. Harry feels guilt when he fights, Billy when he refuses to fight. If Mr. Doe fails to be super-strict on his children, he experiences guilt—even though unknown to him it is best for his children that he be not so strict.

This distinction between adequate and inadequate opinions of what is right reproduces a distinction between what I call *false guilt* and *legitimate guilt*. False guilt results from a poor opinion of rightness and legitimate guilt from a proper opinion.

The Ultimate Standard for Rightness

So far I have used guilt as the psychologist does. But when a lawyer speaks of guilt, he has no reference at all to feelings of guilt—he is speaking of an objective legal guilt. The criminal is legally guilty of his crime whether he suffers guilt feelings or not. Similarly a moralist speaks of guilt with no consideration of whether the morally guilty person experiences feelings of guilt at all. What I consider a legitimate psychological guilt is one that accompanies legal and moral guilt, assuming the civil laws and moral code by which legal and moral guilt are determined are what they should be.

The question remains, How can an adequate moral code be specified? By what criterion can we judge whether our opinions of right and wrong are adequate or poor?

A criterion often pointed to is the persons-are-important standard. Whatever is best for persons has greatest moral merit and should be considered as right. Evil consists exclusively in using persons as things.

This humanistic standard of value, however, is broad enough to allow an innocent person to be forced to death in order to spare twenty guilty persons. By the persons-are-important standard, putting the innocent person to death is the right thing to do because a larger number of persons have been spared even though they were morally or legally guilty.

Further, in many moral confrontations other persons are not involved at all. I may tell a flat lie about my age when it will not bring the least hurt or harm to any other person on earth. Does truth have nothing to do with what is right? There are many situations in which God would be definitely displeased and his righteousness offended by my action when it is not otherwise damaging or abusive at all. The persons-are-important standard is not anti-Christian, for Christianity teaches persons are important. But it is sub-Christian. It is inadequate as a criterion for moral rightness in a distinctively Christian ethic.

Closely related to the persons-are-important standard is the needs-of-society standard, which also is humanistic. Instead of being an act against God, sin is considered merely antisocial behavior. God's laws have been replaced with rules of social value. Since man results from evolution rather than God's creation, human life is no longer sacred. Thus both fascist and communist governments have been created which see man's primary importance to be service to the state. Six million Jews were undesirable to a Nazi regime and were exterminated. We cringe, but the needs-of-society standard gives us no basis to recoil from such barbarism.

The persons-are-important and the needs-of-society standards, assuming they are adequate criteria for moral value, pose another question that just will not go away. It is as simple as this: What makes persons and social structures so important? The only answer that is ultimately adequate is that persons are created by God for his purpose. This gives human life sanctity, sacredness and significance. About the only other option is that man is more important to me than an animal because he is of *my* kind and I respect my kind. Such a self-centered reason for considering man significant does not give man any importance beyond himself. He is not important, period; he is important only *to me*, as a horse may be important to another horse and a chimpanzee to another chimp.

When we admit that man is important because he is created by God for his purpose, we by this very admission are also admitting there is a higher standard of morality than persons-are-important. The character of God, the will of God, the purposes of God—these become criteria for what is right and what is wrong. An ethic that is genuinely Christian makes God not only the source of moral order but also the standard of moral rightness. This means there are certain absolute standards conforming to the will of God with which man is morally responsible to comply. These may be thoughtlessly disparaged as church dogma, but some of us are convinced that God has gone to great care to establish certain absolute principles. These we consider revealed. It is not a dogma to be accepted by faith alone, but a conclusion arrived at by what we think are our Adult minds after carefully considering the alternatives.

With this background we can see in the following chapter how our feelings of guilt can adequately be handled from a Christian point of view.

6

HOW TO HANDLE GUILT

*A*s damaging and devastating as a nagging, gnawing sense of guilt is to the human personality, it would be even more fatal to attempt to eliminate this not-OKness in the wrong way. Many approaches to the problem of guilt blindly assume that all guilt is bad and any way to remove it is acceptable.

It should first be realized, however, that guilt is not the worst thing in the world, and when guilt is either eliminated or prevented at the expense of risking a worse situation, the price is too high. Committing murder is more damaging than feeling guilty, for instance, and it would not be proper to consider murder to be right simply to prevent the guilt that might emerge from committing the crime. A notorious murderer recently justified his act on the grounds of divine orders. If the criminal were genuinely convinced that "God told me to do it," the crime was accompanied by no feelings of guilt because the murder to him was the right thing to do.

It would be dangerous indeed to consider all killing to be all right in order simply to prevent the guilt that otherwise would follow. This is also true of many actions that are less obvious than committing murder.

Second, we should realize that legitimate guilt can be healthy and helpful. Not all guilt is inherently bad. It may be bad for the personality, but if handled correctly it can work for ultimate good. Legitimate guilt stands as a deterrent against committing destructive and harmful acts; it is to the soul what pain is to the body—an alarm signal that warns of danger. Legitimate guilt has merit in correcting a person after he has done wrong and motivating him to seek to rectify his wrong deed. And it is beneficial in making the OKness of God's forgiveness a real incentive that can lead a person into a relationship with God.

Redefining Right and Wrong

From what we now understand about guilt we can easily see three options in attempting to handle it. First, by examining and evaluating our opinions of what is right and wrong, *our Adult can redefine the categories of right and wrong*.

Earlier I said that these opinions ordinarily come from cultural conditioning, from training, from the body of recorded data. But this does not mean that a person is a helpless product of his environment with no power of his own to determine what is right. Though the Parent is the passive recipient of its opinions, the Adult for the mature person is capable of scrutinizing these opinions and redefining what is right. Mr. John Doe has an Adult that can reeducate his Parent about how to rear his children, and he need no longer feel guilty when granting them a measure of freedom. While being influenced by his conditioning, the mature person has freedom in his Adult beyond the limitations of his past teaching to form new opinions of rightness conformable with reality as he sees it.

Here, however, a great danger is lurking: The new ideas of what is right must be formed with greatest caution. Unless the Adult is dead honest in using the standards for moral rightness discussed in the last chapter, the Parent may be given new opinions just as warped as the original.

Rightness can be defined so broadly and wrongness so narrowly that "anything goes." Persons are hurt both financially and emotionally, and it is covered with the notion that "it was a business deal." Both our business ethics and our personal morality become outright anti-Christian, and they are "right" because "everybody's doing it." The most popular approach to guilt today is rationalization, twisting the truth until we are comfortable with it. The category of what is right becomes so broad that nothing is wrong, and the legitimate guilt is eliminated along with the false guilt. It is a fatal mistake to seek to abolish the healthy guilt by making almost everything right and nothing wrong. The reevaluation of one's opinions of what is right must be undertaken only by an Adult scale of values that takes into consideration the Christian absolutes as well as the importance of persons.

There are those today, however, who suffer from false guilt, sometimes called an exaggerated or oversensitive conscience. It results from too narrow an opinion of what is right. Almost everything is wrong. The category of right things is not large enough to accommodate the individual who has been created as a human being to live on a planet called Earth in a society of earthlings. He is trying to wear a suit several sizes too small, and he is in a strait jacket. He is perfectionistic—bound by rules and regulations that imprison him—and he cannot function as a normal person. He is suffering from claustrophobia of compunctions.

The Adult needs to redefine for the Parent what is right and what is not, according to Christian standards. By giving new data to the Parent, the opinions of what is right can be changed until the person has elbow room to be a real person. The false guilt that was suffocating him is removed, and he has breathing room again. This is real freedom!

Killing the Conscience

This only shows us, however, how to be OK from false guilt. The other two methods of handling guilt deal with legitimate guilt. So the second option in handling guilt is simply to *allow the sense of moral oughtness to grow dull.*

This is a dangerous thing to do on two counts. First, a lot of guilt is going to sift down into the subconscious Child while the conscience is becoming dull, and this guilt will eventually erupt in the form of fear or hate. And second, it is dangerous because the conscience becomes incapacitated to be a guiding force in life. Man ceases to be an active moral person when he develops an immunity to guilt. The Controlling Parent dies. The conscience becomes like a cracked bell; it rings false. The person becomes morally dead in a moral universe.

It is like putting a stopper in your ear for so long that you lose your hearing or covering your eye with a bandage so long that you lose your sight. A person's ear can be closed to the voice of God so long that he cannot hear him. His eyes can be closed to truth so long that he cannot recognize it.

He becomes a moral corpse in a morally alive world, and for him there are no "vibrations" of conscience. The Parent is lost as a restraining, directing, steadying force in life.

An American Indian once said, "Conscience is a little three-cornered thing inside me. When I do wrong it turns around and hurts me very much, but if I keep on doing wrong it turns so much that the corners come off and it doesn't hurt me any more."

A person can live so close to the junk pile so long that he no longer smells it. He can live contrary to his conscience so long that the "little light in the soul" grows dim and then goes out. He can take oughtness so lightly for so long that he is immunized by the inoculation. The apostle Paul speaks of "a good conscience" (1 Tim. 1:5) but he also speaks of those who have "their conscience seared with a hot iron" (1 Tim. 4:2, AV).

This second way of handling guilt is too high a price to pay. One sacrifices too much when he loses his Parent and dies morally simply to eliminate the feeling of guilt.

Confessing Your Sin: Three Steps

The third way of handling guilt is to *confess to God the sin that caused the guilt and to accept the OKness from his forgiveness.* Christianity teaches that Jesus, in a way not fully comprehensible and certainly not exhaustible by the rational mind of man, absorbed the sins of the world when he died for man on the cross. He became the victim of our sins, and in his death he reconciled infinite justice with divine mercy.

Some psychologists object by saying that guilt cannot be transferred from one person to another. Of course, they are correct. Christianity claims not that Jesus took our psychological guilt but that he took our legal guilt. He took the kickback, the fallout, the repercussion of our sins. On the basis of his innocent death God forgives our sins, so that the psychological guilt, the feelings of guilt in the Child, can dissolve.

There are three steps in this Christian approach to guilt. The first is an Adult *confession*—a confession of sin. Karl Menninger, the eminent psychiatrist, has asked the question in the title of his recent book, *What Ever Became of Sin?* When a person confesses that he has sinned, he is confessing his offense was against God, for sin by definition means against God. If the sin is recognized as against God, it must be confessed to God, realizing he is the only one in a position to offer utter forgiveness. King David confessed, "I have sinned against the LORD" (2 Sam. 12:13).

A lot has been said about the "crushing implications" of admitting guilt. Indeed, it is difficult for the Child to admit being not-OK—the nature of the Child is to pretend OKness to cope with not-OK feelings. Confession of sin, however, is terribly crushing to the Child *only* when there is nothing to latch onto. It is not so crushing to admit being not-OK *if* one can hold onto the OKness of Christ. When the Adult has confidence in God's forgiveness, this confidence furnishes the Child with an OKness even in the confession of not-OKness—an OKness that has its source beyond the OKness of the world. The confession of not-OKness (guilt) is a healthy confession only when it is made by the Adult. It becomes a practical confession that squares with reality rather than a pressurized emotional confession that crushes the Child with not-OKness. There is a catharsis, a new OKness, an emotional cleansing for the Child from an Adult confession of sin that one cannot experience by suppressing the guilt and pretending the offense was not a sin. When the Adult confesses moral guilt to God, the Child is in a position to experience a purifying freedom from the psychological guilt.

Confession of sin committed against God cannot be an act of ritual taken lightly. When Jesus died under the weight of our sins, it was a life-and-death matter. Repeated shallow confession made superficially falls far short of Christian confession. Christian confession includes a willingness to make special effort to eliminate the acts of sinning, an effort which is often called *repentance*.

This confession amounts to pleading guilty before God and requesting mercy. A refusal to confess is to ask for justice, and this closes mercy out. An innocent person does not need mercy—he needs justice. But we have sinned, we are morally guilty, and the last thing we need is justice. If we should get what we justly deserved there would be no hope. A Hebrew proverb says, "He who conceals his transgressions will not prosper, but he who confesses and forsakes them will obtain mercy" (Prov. 28:13).

The second step is to *accept forgiveness from God*. Sometimes this divine forgiveness may be felt immediately by the Child, but whether the Child feels it or not, it should be intentionally and thoughtfully received by the Adult. God has promised in Holy Scripture to forgive those who come to him in repentance. We believe his promise with our Adult minds, and we accept his forgiveness with an Adult faith. The Child is released from its enslaving guilt—the sin is forgiven and forgotten—and there is no reason to feel guilty.

It is at this point that the relationship with God is established. The sins that separated from God are forgiven, and the guilt that prevented the restoration of that relationship is removed. When Jesus died on the cross to forgive, he was reaching one hand to a holy God and the other toward a sinning human, and in his own death he plugged the human into God. The alienation is overcome by his reconciliation. The short-circuited relationship is repaired, and the detached person is reconnected. He has a relationship with God that is not distorted with guilt!

Now that the guilt that made the Child not-OK is removed, new recordings for a renewed Parent are received from living out the relationship with God.

The third step is to *forgive yourself*. When God has forgiven your sins, your Adult can turn off the condemning recordings of Controlling Parent and turn on the forgiving recordings of Nurturing Parent. Your Adult switches from your accusing Parent to your accepting Parent because God accepts you and no longer condemns you. God has taken away the ammunition for your Controlling Parent by forgiving your offenses. You understand with your Adult that you have no reason to condemn yourself now that you are forgiven. It may take awhile for the Adult to free the Child from the feelings of guilt and condemnation, especially if that feeling has become a habitual pattern. But the Parent is now equipped with forgiveness for the Child, and with this equipment the Adult in time can free the Child from its pattern of guilt. The Child is OK with the Parent because it is OK with God.

The Adult has eliminated the false guilt in the Child by furnishing the Parent with a set of truth data that allows only legitimate guilt. Now the Adult has equipped the

Parent to handle the legitimate guilt in the Child because the offenses that caused the guilt are forgiven.

Until now we have talked of the Child and Parent and how each relates to the Adult. In the following chapter we zoom in on the Adult more specifically to understand what we have assumed up to this point—that the Adult has an element of initiative and creativity capable of choosing to act one way or another, thus making a person responsible for the action he chooses.

7

IS MAN RESPONSIBLE?

Many persons with only a scant exposure to Transactional Analysis grossly misinterpret the primary thrust of the system. The Parent, Child and Adult are seen as products of recorded data for which one is not responsible. Personal behavior is blamed on the "person" within, which is blamed on recorded data (conditioning from the past), which is blamed on causes beyond one's control. A cause-and-effect chain is set up that locks a person's behavior inside a deterministic system. Parent, Child and Adult are understood as character conditions which are determined exclusively by past events called data recordings, and these character conditions exclusively determine a person's behavior.

The buck is passed to the "person" within who is expected to take the rap for whatever one does. No place is left for the personal freedom of the agent, and hence there is no way to assign personal responsibility to the one who performs the behavioral acts. All the blame is pinned on a prior cause. This attempt to unravel the TA method comes out at a diametrically opposite position to what Transactional Analysis really teaches.

Suppose a neighbor complains that my lawn is not mowed and my hedges are not trimmed. My Child wishes to express reaction and my Parent attempts to inhibit reaction. A conflict emerges between my Child and Parent, between the alternatives of expression and inhibition. The philosophical determinists and psychological behaviorists expect me to act according to whichever comes on stronger at the moment, my Child or my Parent. I become the helpless victim of my data recordings, and I am not free to act differently. Consequently, I am not responsible for what I do—I neither deserve praise or reward for responsible acts nor blame or punishment for irresponsible acts. Libertarians in philosophy, however, have long contended for an element of freedom within the agent himself—a freedom to choose *between* the conflicting options within one's personality and also a freedom to choose *beyond* one's own character traits. Now the Transactional Analysts have objectified this freedom in terms of an Adult. The Adult, according to TA, occupies a unique position of umpire over the Parent-Child conflict.

Man: Determined or Free

There are five basic alternate answers to the problem of determinism and freedom. The first contends that a strict mechanistic determinism is true, and man is thus left with no freedom. He is a robot, a machine. Every word in Shakespeare's *Hamlet* was a result of many causal continua all converging on Shakespeare's pen at the same time. Even though Shakespeare chose to write as he did, his choosing was predetermined by past influences and data recordings so that he did not choose freely. He had choice, but it was enslaved choice, not free choice. In TA terms, this view would hold that each person has a Child and a Parent, but no Adult—or if he has an Adult, it has no element of freedom.

Many psychologists in this tradition fail to distinguish between human action and mere human movement. They place both together without distinction under the heading of human behavior. They see no difference between the active and the passive, between acting and being acted upon, between I-do-it and it-is-done-in-me. This view leaves no room for difference between automobile movement and human action; both are caused by events within the agent but beyond the control of the agent.

The second alternative is that determinism is false and freedom is true. The difficulty with this is that without determinism of sorts (efficient causation) man could not in any way determine or cause his own action. Human behavior is then nothing but chance, and man is still not free.

The third option is summed up in the phrase "causation without compulsion." David Hume, Jonathan Edwards and P. H. Nowell-Smith, for example, hold that freedom and determinism are compatible in that the agent can be free from compulsion without being free from causation. The word *agent* is understood in terms of character inclinations, dispositions and mental states (which we are calling Child and Parent); these are determined by outside causes (data recordings) beyond the person's control. The agent himself, however, is considered free in that he can act in accordance with his own character. Praise and blame, rewards and punishment, are considered useful as being corrective or educative in changing human character in an ethic of consequences.

The difficulty here is that there is no genuine freedom. The person's freedom to act is like the freedom of the hands of a clock to move over the clock's face. The freedom is an illusion in that the clock hands are under exact control. The person's choices for action are under exact control of causes within his character over which he has no control. The Adult chooses, but it is only free to choose according to its own preformed character. There are no real options.

The fatal result is that moral responsibility is assigned to a person for what he could not help. He had no alternatives and therefore could not be morally responsible. Moral praise and blame become futile. Punishment is misplaced, unjust and cruel.

The only way "causation without compulsion" can be plausible is by allowing the cause to be an insufficient cause of the action rather than sufficient. That is, the cause is influential rather than determinative, or, we might say, *a* determinant rather than *the* determinant. But this leaves plenty of room for the element of free creative choice which this view is not prepared to allow.

A fourth option holds that the additional element of *intention* serves to distinguish human action from mechanical movement, and with this a person has freedom without having to posit a break in causal continuity. Here we have two kinds of causes—an efficient cause which has to do with motives and character inclinations found in the Child and Parent, and a final cause which has to do with purposes and intentions found in the Adult. Both the motive and intention are considered necessary, and together they are sufficient for action.

However, we can easily see situations in which a person has both the motive and intention to act but never acts. Both prior mental states (motives) and intentions toward future goals together are inadequate causes without some added event to produce the action. There is a difference between *motives to act* and *motivated acts*, and the difference is the action. When we say Jones *intentionally does* something, we are talking about two things—the intention and the doing. We do not say intentions moved the hand; we say the person moved the hand intentionally. The intention explains the purpose or goal of the movement, but it does not explain the cause or source of the movement.

Similarly, motives are inadequate to explain the source of movement because they do not explain why the action occurred *when* it did. Indeed, the motive may be present without the act ever being performed. Then too, it cannot be shown that the same action always follows the same motive or mental state. There are occasions when a person acts "out of character," when the action seems not to be compatible with the state of a person's character at all.

There are also times when intentions are formed that are not in the least subject to one's desires or motives, intentions that are totally different from the desires. But even if prior character states should adequately explain the forming of intentions, they still have not explained the translating of intentions into actions. The source of movement still has not been explained. Intentions and character condition together leave a missing link in the analysis of human action.

In order to explain *acting* and *doing* we must point to an *actor* and *do-er*, for the notions of acting and doing presuppose actor and do-er in a way that makes the notions otherwise unintelligible. So again we are pushed back to the Adult to look for a missing link—to look for a power to originate the movement.

Autonomous Man

The fifth alternative allows for both determinism and freedom in a way that avoids the previous contradictions and makes responsibility a very plausible notion. Here the Adult stands in a privileged position which gives it freedom to form intentions by deciding *between* the motives of Child and Parent, in which case the person is said to *formulate* his intentions. The Adult is also in a position, at least in certain instances, to choose *beyond* the motives of Child and Parent, in which case the person is said to *originate* his intentions. This accounts for the fact that persons often form intentions different from either the desires of their Child or Parent.

To say that the Adult is in such a unique privileged position is simply to say that there belongs to the Adult the *capacity* to initiate an intention to act. This is a negative idea, meaning the Adult is *free from* the restraints of a prior determinism. This capacity, however, can be developed into a *capability*, an active power, to transfer the intention into action. This is a positive idea, meaning the Adult is *free to* use causation (or determinism) to cause (or determine) an action. If man were only *free from* determinism without being *free to* determine, his behavior would be pure random or chance rather than human action.

Stated another way, there is a break in the causal continuity, in the cause-and-effect chain, so that a person's Adult is free *from* causation and free *to* initiate causation in an otherwise mechanistically and psychologically determined world. Being both undetermined and determinative, the Adult has the creative power to produce an action. Like a small god, man is a "prime mover unmoved." He has an element of creative autonomy that enables him to determine in a way that is undetermined and thus is a cause uncaused. He has a freedom that is "freer" than "caused by character."

This is obviously not to say that a person is free from circumstantial limitations, only free within these limitations. And it is not to say that his actions are never caused by the motives in his Child and Parent, only that his actions need not be controlled by his Child and Parent.

The Adult represents both the "thought" concept of life with the power to think through a situation and also the "will" concept of life with the power to choose between viable alternatives. Man's free will then is not thought of as a faculty of human personality, but as an active power to perform an act, as different from a passive capacity to move when moved upon. This power is a precondition for action but not a faculty or mental state. "Choosing" and "willing" are verb forms that describe the exercising of the power to perform an act. It is the Adult, rather than the Parent or Child, that acts.

Responsible Man

With such an autonomous Adult, the notion of being responsible in the sense of being *accountable* is easily understood. Being responsible in the sense of being *dependable* is perfectly compatible with psychological determinism, for a person can be expected to act according to his own set character. But with a creative Adult, a person is accountable because he has the freedom to act beyond the set and mold of his own motives, dispositions and character. Punishment is still intended to be corrective, but it is nevertheless justified because the punishment is deserved. Man is morally responsible for his actions because he was free to accept, reject or change his course of action, and the notions of deserved reward and justified punishment are valid concepts.

With a creative, autonomous Adult, man is responsible for *choosing* freely a relationship with God as well as making other appropriate choices in life. Thomas Harris interprets God's grace as God saying to man, "You're OK," not "You can be OK *if* . . ."[1] This is to say that our being accepted by God is not predicated upon anything that we do—that grace is unconditional. This is certainly true from God's point of view. Forgiveness is free and cannot be bargained for.

It must be remembered, however, that sin (a concept which will be explained later), while not making God exclude us, makes us exclude him. The sin of choosing not to relate to God is equivalent to rejecting his grace. It is writing God off, writing moral rightness off, shutting out divine love. It is true that God does not say, "I will accept you only *if* you repent (turn from self to God)," but he does say, "You can only receive and experience my acceptance if you repent." The notion of "receiving" God without "repenting" is contradictory, for the first includes the second. Man is in no position to receive God's pronouncement of OKness until he freely chooses to be OK with God.

Earlier in the book we have seen how the Adult is equipped with the power to examine and reason. In this chapter we have seen how the Adult is equipped with the power to choose freely. With these two pieces of equipment life situations can be handled adequately. Before we look more specifically at how this can be done, we need to see in the next chapter how the Adult capacity to choose and act can be developed into an active power and how the Adult can be bolstered and built into a positive, creative force in one's life

8

FREEING THE ADULT

A college student whose lifestyle had become a perilous maelstrom of danger came to my office for counsel. Knowing she was on a collision course, Pam was disturbed about the direction and destiny of her life. As an amateur psychologist, she considered herself a specialist in diagnosing all the causes of her own problems. She pointed to the rearing her parents had given her, hereditary traits in her nature, childhood experiences, a failure on the part of the church and a God who did not seem to care. She blamed society, the political establishment and the laws of the land. It never seemed to have occurred to Pam that she at least in part might be responsible for some of her own problems.

I pointed out that no one ever had a perfect rearing, that her parents had parents too, and their parents had parents. I explained that she could not point to some quirk in her past and make it responsible for what she is today, that she is not responsible for where she came from but where she is going. I showed her how so many others had risen above an unsatisfactory background and had made the most of a situation they could not change. Wanting me to prescribe a simple capsule to resolve her dilemma, not once was Pam willing to accept any of the responsibility for her predicament.

What Pam had done was this: She had catered to her Child so long that her Adult (and probably her Parent also) was "contaminated" with her Child and partially blocked out. With such an inactive Adult, Pam voluntarily had become a slave to her Child. Her Adult still had the capacity for free choice, but it was not operating as an active power. The two pieces of Adult equipment—a rationality for examining the situation objectively and a power to make appropriate choices in spite of the situation—were deactivated.

Another situation is illustrated by a young man rooming at the YMCA in Louisville. Denny came to one of our evangelades and cornered me for a session after the service. "I tell myself that when I'm with my gang I'll not talk their obscenities, racial slurs and profanities," he said. "But I always crumble under the pressure of the crowd." And he added, "It's all my fault. I just won't do what I know I should do."

By coming to me Denny was admitting that he needed help, that he alone could not do what he knew he should do. Yet in his confession he was saying that the only reason he *could* not was that he *would* not, realizing that he could if he would. The problem then was a matter of his will, his choice. In this case, Denny had a partially active Adult—he still understood the situation. Yet his Adult had been contaminated by the Child until his Adult was impaired. The second piece of Adult equipment—the power to make the appropriate choice—was deactivated.

With both Pam and Denny, the Adult needed to be emancipated from the prejudices of the Parent and the emotional desires of the Child so that the Adult could function with both its rational examination of situations and its power to choose appropriately.

The question that follows is this: How can an inactive Adult be activated? How can the Adult's capacity for free choice be developed into an active power? How can the contaminated Adult be emancipated from the Child and Parent to regain its autonomy and creative activity?

Getting into Gear–Reverse, That Is

First, though poor data recordings may account for a part of Adult weakness, the chances are pretty high that the Adult became contaminated by abdicating its own privileged position and relinquishing its prerogatives a little at a time. Choosing to accommodate the Child or Parent becomes a habitual pattern until the Child or Parent gains control over the weakened Adult. When the Parent gains control, the Adult loses its ability to examine the situation rationally and the result is prejudice. When the Child gains control, the Adult loses its power of creative choice and the result is uncontrolled passion, or temper or obsessions.

If the Adult became contaminated by a series of inappropriate choices accommodating the Child, *the Adult becomes emancipated by reversing the trend and reestablishing its privileged position through a series of appropriate choices*. The Adult can reassert its executive prerogatives until it becomes a pattern. This is simply to say that many persons are so accustomed to obliging their Child that they are out of practice making responsible choices. They simply need to get in practice. Unless a person is psychotic or psychopathic, he has enough of the Adult left to reassert itself—even though it may have been contaminated and deactivated for a period.

It is the person with no rational or free element in the Adult at all who is unable to regain an appropriate control of his responses in pressure-packed situations. The Adult is completely blocked out and decommissioned. Because there is no element of freedom, he is not considered responsible for his actions—nor is he held legally culpable by our courts. A kleptomaniac is not accountable for his action even though he caused the action because he was not free *not* to perform the action. His Adult autonomy is lost. Shoplifting for the genuine kleptomaniac should be considered unsocial behavior rather than action for which he is morally responsible.

Most persons, however, have enough of an Adult to begin a series of Adult choices that will make further Adult choices come more easily.

Decontaminating the Adult

Second, *an adequate relationship with God helps to emancipate the Adult from the prejudices of the Parent and the desires of the Child.* In fact, it is really impossible for many persons to have a decontaminated Adult without the God-relationship because they are hopelessly wrapped up in themselves. They have nothing far enough beyond themselves to capture their commitment, until they are lifted out of themselves by a meaningful relationship with God.

This is so much the case that the New Testament teaches the contaminated Adult is unable to come to God for forgiveness and acceptance until given added power. Jesus said, "No one can come to me, except the Father . . . draws him" (Jn. 6:44). Yet even here man is without excuse, for "the grace of God has appeared for the salvation of all men" (Tit. 2:11). God has taken the initiative to touch man on his own level, not waiting for man to rise to meet God on his level. And James promised, "Draw near to God and he will draw near to you" (Jas. 4:8).

In earlier chapters we have seen what a relationship with God can do for the Parent and Child. It gives the Child both the security of belonging, which eliminates the not-OKness of estrangement, and the security of meaning, which eliminates the not-OKness of worthlessness. The Child is thus relieved from a large part of its not-OKness.

The God-man relationship supplies truth data for the Parent's opinions of what is right, thus alleviating false guilt in the Child. The Child is relieved from another large portion of its not-OKness. Then the relationship with God provides forgiveness and release from the genuine guilt, thus alleviating still another large part of the Child's not-OKness.

It is the not-OK Child that contaminates and excludes the Adult, not the OK Child. After the relationship with God has been established, there are other areas in which the Child feels not-OK, especially those areas of human relationships. But with such a large part of the not-OKness removed and such a large area of OKness established by the God-relationship, the Adult is quite naturally freed from much of the contamination imposed by the Child's not-OKness. When Christ makes my Child OK by forgiveness and acceptance, then my Adult is free from the enslaving entanglements with my Child. Jesus said, "I tell you the truth: everyone who sins is a slave of sin. . . . If the Son makes you free, then you will be really free" (Jn. 8:36, TEV).

The Spirit Is Willing

Third, the relationship with God not only helps free the Adult from the restrictions imposed by Child and Parent, Scripture teaches and experience confirms that *the God-man relationship actually gives new power to the Adult*. A supernatural force is released in the human personality, and the Adult begins to transcend its own power and draw resources from beyond itself. There is an inner deposit of new strength. Moral braces are built into the character.

There may be "religious" experiences without the supernatural element, but *Christian* experience requires the presence of Christ for its explanation. The change that results in the human personality may be explained in psychological terms and personality structures, but the presence of Christ cannot be scientifically explained. The divine Presence is supernaturally given, and it fortifies the Adult's creative power of choice.

The Holy Spirit himself comes to live within the personality structures, and with him he brings the presence of Christ.

To the apostle Paul, Jesus said, "My grace is sufficient for you, for my power is made perfect in weakness." And Paul responded, "When I am weak, then am I strong" (2 Cor. 12: 9-10). Again Paul said, "I can do all things in him [Christ] who strengthens me" (Phil. 4:13). And again, "My God will supply every need of yours according to his riches in glory in Christ Jesus" (Phil. 4:19).

No man is so free—free from the bondage of Child and Parent, and with a supernatural additive to reinforce the Adult—as the person who has a real and genuine relationship with God. With this free power in the Adult, life situations can be handled adequately, as we shall see in the chapters that follow.

9

MAINTAINING THE RELATIONSHIP

"What happened to me?" Jerry asked, with disappointment and defeat written across his face. I had just given an address in Pennsylvania when the teen-ager came to the corner where I stood, gave his shoulder-length hair a fling with a twist of his head and stared at me through eyes filled half with disgust, half with hope.

Jerry was a new Christian, recently having placed his confidence in Jesus Christ for a relationship with God. He had felt a deep sense of acceptance, forgiveness and belonging. At times he had been almost overwhelmed with feelings of relief and new joy. The drudgery and monotony of life had seemed far behind. Life was so sweet and good that he somehow had expected to stay "high" the rest of his life.

Then it happened. Jerry had to return to Planet Earth to live. Life became humdrum as he faced the hard grind. The usual teen-age temptations became frustrating, at times almost suffocating, closing in on him so that he could not beat them back. He felt a sense of isolation when his old friends did not understand his new commitment. He began to wonder how his life with Christ should be lived out, and he was gripped with anxieties about his future. Life began to seem harsh and cruel and cold.

Up to this point everything was pretty normal and on schedule. The fatal mistake was when Jerry began to say to himself, "What happened to my relationship with God? It doesn't feel like it once did." Discouragement set in, followed by mild depression. And the confidence in Christ was almost undermined.

It is the same old story of the Child being in control—this time deactivating the Adult's power of reasonable examination rather than the power of choice. It was the Child that experienced the immediate benefit of the relationship with God. The Child had felt estranged from God and worthless. Now it felt the security of belonging and meaningfulness. The Child had felt guilt and rebuke, and now it felt forgiveness, acceptance and approval. The Child had felt not-OK and now it felt OK with God.

Jerry's mistake came in getting his attention focused on the *feeling* that resulted from the relationship rather than on the *fact* of the relationship. Thus the Child's position in the total personality usurped the position of the Adult, pre-empting an Adult understanding of the nature of the relationship. When the Child feeling began to subside, what had been understood as the basic ingredient of the relationship seemed to be gone. Jerry had nothing to latch onto.

The relationship with God is primarily something to be understood and cultivated by the Adult rather than something to be felt by the Child. The Child feeling is not to be disparaged, but it is not to be elevated to the primary ingredient. The feeling is to be understood by the Adult as a useful by-product of the relationship.

More specifically, in its privileged position of examining and choosing, the Adult can understand two things about the God-man relationship. With this understanding the Child becomes free to enjoy its feeling and is given the confidence of OKness even when the intensity of feeling abates.

Fact, Faith and Feeling

First, *the Adult can understand the fluctuation pattern of emotion.* The level of emotional intensity in any normal person is quite naturally characterized by an ebb and flow. This variety is necessary for emotional health. Sustained ecstasy puts a heavy strain on the nervous system and eventually may result in extreme neurosis or even psychosis.

For normal persons the level of feeling fluctuates back and forth across the level of norm, usually falling about the same distance below as it had arisen above. This is why those who are given to easy ecstasy are ordinarily the ones who are most vulnerable to depression. It is often the case also that the longer a person's emotions remain above the level of norm, the longer they will stay below when they fall.

When this fluctuation pattern is understood, the Adult is equipped to handle the situation when the Child has less feeling from the relationship with God than he had at another time. The Adult even anticipates such a "let down" and is prepared for it when it happens. Someone said, "I feel just as good when I don't feel good as I feel when I do feel good because I know I will feel good again later on."

This is the Adult understanding the Child's feelings rather than being overwhelmed by those feelings.

A couple of generations ago an uneducated, diseased, poverty-stricken young man was converted one night in an old-fashioned tent meeting. Bud Robinson was so excited about it that the stars seemed to dance all over the sky as he walked the country road back home after service. When he awoke the following morning his emotions had leveled off, and he actually thought the devil had slipped inside his open window and stolen away his religion. Later he learned how undependable his emotions really were, and "Uncle Buddy" became a favorite American preacher whose influence encircled the globe.

Some persons are always feeling of their feelings to feel how their feelings are feeling. And they often feel that their feelings are not feeling as good as their feelings were feeling the last time they felt of their feelings to feel how their feelings were feeling. They take their spiritual temperature by their emotional pulse and appraise their relationship with God by the way they feel at the moment. Obviously any person's relationship with God would be pretty precarious if it rested on such a tenuous foundation as feeling.

It is exercising Adult responsibility to realize that no meaningful relationship in life rests primarily on Child emotion, but on Adult effort. The fellowship between any two personalities is quite normally characterized by the ebb and flow without affecting their relationship.

This is true in the stability of a husband-wife relationship. My Sheila and I have a beautiful and meaningful personal relationship. There are moments of intense feelings of love, transparent joy, and a oneness of spirit. There are other moments when the feeling subsides to little more than a quiet assurance. The feelings are simply the side effects of the relationship which remains constant regardless of the ebb and flow of the feelings. The relationship is the deep continuous current while the feelings are the rippling waves that rise and fall on the surface.

If my only assurance of being married rested on my feelings, much of my time would be spent wondering whether I am married. The truth is that much of the time I do not even feel married. It is not that I ever feel unmarried; at times I just do not feel either way. Sometimes I am not even thinking about being married and consequently I do not feel at all about being married. But I know I am a married man because one night I stood before the marriage altar. The clergyman said, "Wilt thou . . . ?" I said, "I will." And he said, "I pronounce you man and wife."

My being married is a *fact* and I believe the fact. I have *faith* in the *fact* regardless of the *feeling*. God has established a relationship with me that is factual regardless of my feeling. The relationship is characterized by the *fact* of my forgiveness, the *fact* of his acceptance of me, the *fact* that he is my Father, the *fact* that I am his son. It is the Child that attempts to reason from the feeling to the fact; the Adult reasons from the fact to the feeling.

By examining the relationship, the mature Adult is capable of distinguishing between the fact, the faith and the feeling, thus furnishing for the Child a confidence making it OK even when the feeling is gone.

In the last few years more books have been published about the Holy Spirit than ever before, signaling an emphasis that is cause for rejoicing among all Christians. Many thousands have experienced the Holy Spirit in their lives, resulting in a broad spectrum of emotional responses. The liability here is that many will proceed to build a theology of Christian experience for everyone else that is based only on their own experience. The truth is that no two spiritual experiences are emotionally identical because each personality is unique. Data recordings for Child and Parent are different for each individual. God has an experience available for each person that is tailor-made for his own personality. The person with a healthy Adult can accept the emotions resulting from his own spiritual experience without expecting them to duplicate those of another.

What God Has Joined Together

Second, *the Adult can understand that it is God who keeps the relationship intact*. Though the needs of my Child and Parent helped lead me to God, it was my Adult that *chose* to respond to the overtures of God, and my Adult chooses to continue this responsiveness. But the initiative was taken by God in the first place. He established the relationship and he is in a position to preserve that relationship. An assurance of the continuing relationship is gained by an Adult faith in the character of God to keep the relationship intact. In time a confidence in the relationship is reached that is hardly affected at all by the ups and downs of the feelings that may be attached to the relationship.

Steve and Mary, a young married couple, have a lovely relationship. Steve works away from home and comes in at evening. Mary can be absolutely sure that Steve is being faithful to their relationship when he is away from home—just as certain as she is when he is in the home. But her confidence rests on an altogether different basis. When he is away it is on the basis of faith in his character and his commitment to her. She does not need so much faith when he is in the home; she can see that he is being faithful.

When you are enjoying the presence of Christ, you do not have to have so much faith for the relationship. The fellowship with God attests the relationship. You have evidence. But when you do not feel his presence, you can still be certain that your relationship with him is intact, but it is on the basis of faith. Someone has said, "Faith is never to forget in the dark what he said to you in the light." Faith is to remember at midnight what you experienced at noonday.

The Adult is able to distinguish between the *feeling* inherent in *fellowship* with God which may fluctuate, and the *faith* inherent in a continuing *relationship* which remains constant because it is preserved by God who originally established it.

When Jerry began to understand this, a new confidence in his God-relationship was gained, and a consequent equilibrium was acquired for fellowship with God. His hit-and-miss prayer life became less haphazard. Now the ebb and flow of personality-interaction is expected. Physical, mental and emotional fatigue are understood to disable the mind only temporarily for concentration and to lower the level of soul-sensitivity for personality-response, affecting his feeling of fellowship rather than God's preservation of the relationship. Participation in the God-personality is more practical and less visionary, more continuous and less spasmodic, more confident and less uneasy. The divine "wave length" is on a practical rather than mystical "frequency."

With relaxation instead of frustration, fellowship with God is now for Jerry a satisfying experience.

The relationship thus maintained, every area of life can be positively affected in a practical way. OKness in the vertical relationship with God makes for an OKness with strong foundation in the horizontal relationships of life, as we shall see in the chapters that remain.

10

PERSONAL PEACE

Mr. Average American (that's me, that's you) is on a journey through life in search of peace. The long quest leads him across battlefields, through combat zones and into bitter confrontations. He fights out civil wars between differing components of his own personality, faces conflicts in his relationships with family, neighbors and business associates, and squares off against the demands of reality, ultimateness and God.

Battered and bruised in these battles of life, his Child gets various feelings ranging all the way from inferiority to superiority. Within the context of these Child feelings, various life positions emerge—I'm OK or I'm not-OK, You're OK or You're not-OK—which are discussed at length by Thomas Harris. It is his contention that the infant very early in life concludes I'm not-OK—You're OK. The result is either an unhealthy acceptance of the position ("Since I'm no good, I'll not even try to be good") or an unhealthy reaction against the position by an exaggerated compulsion to achieve.

The Abnormality of Not-OKness

It is my contention that a person would be able to accept the I'm not-OK—You're OK position in life without reacting so unhealthily if it were his normal psychological habitat. But man has been created for ultimate purposes that make his life important, and this leaves him forever unable to accept a position which to him is abnormal. Being created for OKness in the universe, man can never be "at home" with not-OKness.

The strong reaction against not-OKness switches man's position to I'm OK—You're not-OK. Here he rationalizes until he flips a mental switch; he convinces himself of his OKness, and to do so he has to switch the other person to not-OKness. His life becomes characterized by a hostility that sustains him and an arrogance that perpetuates his own OKness. We even see evidences of this position in very small children.

Here we see a valid distinction between the "normal" and the "natural"—between the normal position for man and the natural position for animal. I'm OK—You're not-OK is necessary for survival in the world of nature. Man, however, belongs essentially to a higher order than the natural, and it is not normal for him to be motivated primarily by criminal animalistic drives. In attempting to overcome the abnormal not-OKness, man sinks to yet a lower level of abnormality by devising You're not-OK—thus identifying with the natural position of the animal. In so doing, man sinks to a lower moral level than animal, for the natural is normal for the animal but not for man. To the animal You're not-OK is amoral, but to man it is immoral.

The animal position, however, is corrected and equalized for the animal by a built-in reality in the world of nature. We call it the law of the jungle, and it is easily recognized and soon accepted by the animal. The animal learns what is stronger than it and what is weaker than it, and it develops feelings of inferiority or superiority true to the reality of the environment. An animal seems to be able to own its true feelings without rationalization, pretension or make belief.

At this point there seems to be a real difference between man and animal. With the I'm OK—You're not-OK position, man develops a self-centeredness he is not quite able to handle. He rationalizes, pretends and makes himself believe he is not inferior to anybody or anything. He develops vanity and haughtiness. And he is unwilling to recognize and accept a position of inferiority, once he has overcome not-OKness with You're not-OK.

Theologically, this unwillingness to accept one's position is what is called the "nature of sin." It is distinguished from committed sins as a noun is different from a verb and as the singular is different from the plural. The nature of sin is the assumed self-centered position in the universe, an arrogance that crowds God out of one's life. It is the unwillingness of the Adult to allow the reality of one's actual position. This exaggerated selfishness may confuse and distort one's central emotional position until he eventually develops the criminal, suicidal position of I'm not-OK—You're not-OK —Everything's not-OK.

Farmer Jackson and Farmer Brown each had a not-OK Child, and they blew their lives in a game of one-upmanship constantly putting the other one down. For each it was a desperate attempt to achieve OKness. When one got a new farm tractor, the other got a more expensive piece of machinery. A feud developed over the land line, then over their children, then over their wives. Neither was willing to accept the other's I'm OK—You're not-OK attitude. The Child in each fought back against being made not-OK by attempting to make the other's Child not-OK. Each refused to be not-OK or to allow the other to be OK. Something somewhere had to give. Eventually Jackson's Child was forced by Brown to admit its not-OKness, but in feeling not-OK he was still unwilling for Brown to feel OK. Jackson was defeated but he refused to surrender. He chose rather to go down fighting. To him everything became not-OK, including himself. One morning Jackson took his shotgun and killed Brown, and then turned and killed himself.

Chances are that an animal would have surrendered when defeated; it would have recognized its defeat and accepted the I'm inferior—You're superior arrangement. But Farmer Jackson, having been made for ultimate OKness, refused to accept an arrangement in which his spirit was not at home. The tension created by his fight and Brown's fight-back made impossible any normal emotional position for Jackson. Brown's selfishness would not allow Jackson's selfishness to have its way. Refusing to resign his selfishness, Jackson was driven to the position of I'm not-OK—You're not-OK—Everything's not-OK. This position is both criminal and suicidal. It is pretty difficult for human selfishness to succeed in a world filled with selfishness all around. For the animal selfishness accedes to a livable arrangement (unless there are added drives), but man's selfishness is often unwilling to make such an accommodation, and it can drive him suicidal.

Man's unwillingness to accept his position of inferiority in the world is a perversion and prostitution of the importance and OKness for which he was created. It results from a misidentification of inferiority with not-OKness and superiority with OKness.

OK in the World

Let's differentiate between two "worlds" occupied by man. One is the world of physical and social contacts. The other is a different dimension of his life, a "world" beyond the physical and visible. It is a world of ultimate desire, eternal dimension and spiritual reality. Paul drew the distinction this way: "The things that are seen are transient, but the things that are unseen are eternal" (2 Cor. 4:18). The one has to do with man's social relationships and the other with his relationship with God. For lack of better terms we will call the first one *world* and the second *universe*.

Now superiority and inferiority are words that ordinarily belong to world while OKness and not-OKness are words which ultimately belong to universe. What we in contemporary society are doing is this: We are attempting to discover OKness by feeling superior; we use the temporal world as a yardstick for the eternal universe. Eternal OKness is sought in a temporary superiority, and only a false, superficial OKness is ever found.

The result is an exaggerated premium on superiority and a false sense of OKness—an OKness that does not reach beyond the immediate situation of superiority. Thus the Child has only a temporary OKness derived from superiority, and the Adult has no further, more permanent OKness to offer the Child.

OK in the Universe

What is not realized is that the universe is so much bigger than the world, the eternal lasts so much longer than the temporal, and there can be a deeper OKness when there is a situation of inferiority. I can feel superiority and yet be basically not-OK, and I can feel inferiority and be basically OK. A wealthy, educated celebrity may feel superior and yet have no OKness beyond his wealth, education and fame. Yet an unknown, uneducated slum dweller can sing, "I may never achieve worldly fame; yet all of heaven can call me by name."

If I am important to God, if I am the object of his love, if I have discovered that he has a purpose for me—then I am OK! I can be accused and ridiculed, and still stand ten feet tall in my own eyes. The person who is OK with God becomes big enough to be willing to look little. It takes a somebody in the universe to be OK as a nobody in the world.

When the world becomes my standard for OKness and I become important by this standard, the logical consequence is that God is not important—or at least that he is irrelevant. Then I am left with no source for OKness beyond the temporal. So I crack my cranium against the reality of the universe in my attempt to be superior in the world. It is a frantic quest for power, popularity, superiority and worldly importance designed to gain a deep OKness which never comes. It is only when God becomes important to us that we understand our importance to him, and thus our importance in the universe. Thus it is only when God counts for everything that man really counts for anything.

It is not difficult to see how genuinely OK persons are humble and the falsely OK, really not-OK, are arrogant, and how the pursuit of OKness in superiority leaves one with the arrogant, self-centered You're not-OK position. Someone said, "Those who reveal a superior exterior often conceal an inferior interior." It is the old story of assuming a superior attitude to compensate for inferior feelings.

It is to this false sense of importance that the "crushing implications of confession" apply. An Adult admission of not-OKness is devastating to egotism, to arrogance, to superficial OKness. And this is exactly what is needed: The ego must be freed from egotism, the Adult emancipated from the Child, the self liberated from self-centeredness. Each layer of false security must be peeled away until we can break out of the closed world system of the Child into the bigger open system of the Adult.

OK with God

When I am OK with God—OK in the universe—my Adult has OKness for my Child even when I am inferior in the world. I have replaced my false security props of worldly importance with the genuine security of being important to God. I can now accept my points of inferiority without either belittling myself or acquiring a false arrogance. I can own my inferiority as a realistic position without relinquishing my OKness. My Child feels inferiority in a healthy, practical way without feeling insecurity and without feeling not-OK. The relationship with God gives me an OKness in the universe that cannot be touched by my inferiority in the world. My Child acquires OK-with-God recordings to which my Adult can switch when my not-OK-in-the-situation recordings are playing.

Building OK feelings by mastering life situations is not to be disparaged, but attempting to gain OKness in the universe by becoming superior in the world is like patching a person up with superficial plaster. Superiority cannot ultimately act as a stand-in for OKness. It leads to arrogance, self-centeredness and sin. And it inevitably leads to the conclusion that the situation or person to whom you are superior is not-OK.

Achieving Personal Peace

What does all this have to do with personal peace? In chapter 1 I spoke of the conflict within the human personality—a conflict between Child and Parent which the Adult has not been able to handle. This tension reflects itself in further social tensions in the community. The secret of real peace is to resolve the inner conflict by integrating and harmonizing the personality under one head.

Let me put it in personal terms. What can I do to bring my own personality under one head? How can I be whole and thus at peace? I have, I believe, four options.

First, I can sell out to my Parent, and I may have a measure of peace, but it is the peace of surrender rather than victory. My life becomes legalistic, strait-jacketed, and my Child remains smothered with guilt.

Or, second, I can surrender to my Child. The problem here is that without a relationship with God my Child is not-OK. To attempt harmony under a not-OK Child is to look for OKness in superiority, to search for peace in power. This is to become vulnerable to the arrogance and hostility of You're not-OK. Peace with my fellowman is totally impossible with the You're not-OK attitude. Tensions develop, hostilities erupt and conflict follows. There is no peace with the not-OK Child in control.

My third alternative is to look for a victorious peace in an Adult chain of command that brings both my Parent and Child into harmony with the decisions of my Adult. A greater measure of peace is possible under this arrangement than the other two. But the problem here is that my Adult is simply not equipped to preside over Parent and Child without a relationship with God.

My Adult's equipment for rational examination is not adequate to define a Christian standard of rightness for my Parent, and my Child is made not-OK by false feelings of guilt. Then without the forgiveness inherent in a God-relationship, my Child is tormented with the not-OKness of genuine guilt. And when my Adult has not discovered ultimate meaning in life, my Child is plagued with the not-OKness of estrangement and purposelessness.

My Child with such not-OKness then contaminates my Adult, deactivating my Adult for appropriate choices. And too, my Adult needs supernatural reinforcement for its free power of choice if it is to be capable of directing both Parent and Child.

But I have a fourth alternative. That is to discover peace in a personal relationship with God chosen by my Adult. My Parent comes into harmony by responding to new truth data for conscience content. My Child is given the security of importance in the universe and no longer needs to master and use others to achieve OKness. Not-OK feelings arising in my Child from recordings of inferiority in the world are understood by my Adult, turned off and easily handled. The relationship with God has freed my Adult from contamination by my Parent and Child, and bolstered my Adult for appropriate choices and intelligent understanding. Thus there is an inner working relationship existing between my Child, Parent and Adult, each functioning in harmony with the other.

There is a cursory peace in surrendering to my Child, but a lasting peace only comes in an Adult-chosen relationship with God. Both Jonah and Jesus slept in the storm for a period, but when they awoke, one could handle the situation and the other could not. For one, the Child was in control and for the other the Adult. Peace is not the absence of disturbance, but the presence of assurance in the disturbance—an assurance that comes by relating to God.

Here we are able to see two kinds of personal peace. The God-relationship first of all gives a person peace *with* God, which is the peace of reconciliation, the peace of belonging, the peace between man and God. This is a peace that mankind throughout recorded history has sought. From this peace with God comes another kind of peace, a peace between the functioning members of the personality. This is the peace *of* God, the peace of inner integration and unification. The variant components of the personality are playing in the same key and directed by the same Conductor.

Paul said, "Since we are justified by faith, we have peace *with* God" (Rom. 5:1). And he also said, "The peace *of* God . . . will keep your hearts and your minds in Christ Jesus" (Phil. 4:7).

11

RELATING TO OTHERS

*H*ere comes Hector. Big, arrogant, always in command, always putting you down. And you can't slip away behind the filing cabinet or down the hall or over in the next aisle. He's seen you. He's heading toward you. You're stuck.

Your biggest problem in relating meaningfully to Hector is not his personality, obnoxious as it may be. It is not his offensive mannerisms or his repugnant ways. The big problem is your own reaction to his personality. If he smiles, you smile; if he frowns, you frown. If he speaks, you speak; if he doesn't, you don't. If he dims his lights, you dim yours; if he doesn't, you flash yours back on high beam!

Jockeying for Position

In the last chapter we saw how our insecure not-OK Child often attempts to gain OKness within the context of this world by making the other person not-OK. "I'm OK because I am superior to you" means "You're not-OK because you are inferior to me." The not-OK Child spends carloads of energy jockeying for position, maneuvering for an advantage over the other person.

It is the nature of Adult to *act* intelligently and decisively, while the nature of not-OK Child is to *react* with childish immaturity. The Adult dims the lights, and the Child brightens the lights to make the oncoming motorist not-OK. The Child feels inadequate (not-OK) in the presence of an uncongenial neighbor, so he becomes snobbish and aloof to make the neighbor feel inadequate (not-OK) around him. Knowing that the neighbor feels inadequate around him gives him a feeling of superiority (OKness).

Relating with persons becomes a defensive battle like a football game. Each one tries to push the other farther back into his own territory in order to wedge out more room for OKness for himself. The line of scrimmage becomes a wall of vindictiveness that precludes any meaningful relationship.

It would be much easier to relate to others if they were all perfect in their action toward me. So I have a couple of options. The first is to undertake the task of making those feel not-OK whose actions are not perfect toward me, thereby making myself feel OK. The second option is to find a more dependable source for my own OKness, thereby relieving myself of the endless frustrating crusade of making others feel not-OK. The first option belongs to the Child, the second to the Adult.

There are almost four billion *other persons* in the world, however, and there is only one *me*. It is so much simpler to control my own attitudes than to engage in the impossible task of controlling everyone else. It is far easier to accept the situation as it is and make the most out of it than to attempt to change the whole situation—a task no one will ever be able to accomplish.

Picture yourself on a hot afternoon highway unable to pass a sightseer who "parks" himself in front of you at a fifteen-mph rate of speed for forty miles. Your Child wants to sit down on the horn to make the culprit feel not-OK. When your Parent inhibits you from sounding the horn, tension begins to build. There is a "tiger in your tank." Your emotions become a pressure cooker, and you do a slow burn. Eventually you arrive at your destination tense and upset, and the man who held up the traffic is relaxed and happy. You have a headache and he feels good!

The problem is with the not-OK Child which contaminates the Adult, usurping its executive position. Paul said, "I do not do what I [Adult] want, but I [Child] do the very thing I [Adult] hate. Now if I [Child] do what I [Adult] do not want . . . , it is no longer I [Adult] that do it, but sin [Child controlling Adult, or Adult giving in to Child] which dwells within me" (Rom. 7:15-17).

When I'm OK with God

The remedy can be found in a relationship with God that gives the Child the security (OKness) of belonging and importance, thus decontaminating the Adult from the not-OK Child and freeing the Adult to regain its executive position for rational understanding and appropriate choices.

This is not to suggest that all problems are immediately and automatically solved by a relationship with God. It is simply to say that *a foundation is established* for solving the problems of interpersonal relationships. The Adult is freed from the not-OK Child and given the power to make decisions creatively, resourcefully and appropriately—to act rather than react to the actions and attitudes of others. By practicing "acting Adult" instead of "reacting Child," the Adult continues to reinforce its executive position further, freeing itself and enlarging its free power of choice. Relating congenially and appropriately with others becomes ever more easy as a pattern of Adult command is established. But the relationship with God gives the basic ingredients for establishing this command.

Inherent in this remedy is the fact that *when the Child is OK with God, it has no fundamental need to make any other person not-OK*. The OK person can allow his neighbor to be OK without affecting his own OKness. He has no reason at all to wish not-OKness for the other person. Jockeying for position is eliminated. The defenses are down.

The ideal situation for meaningful relationships is when both parties are OK, neither therefore attempting to maneuver the other to not-OKness.

Perfect provision is made for this kind of relationship within Christian marriage, which has the potential for the most beautiful paradise this side of heaven. Husband and wife do not relate meaningfully in either a husband-dominated or a wife-dominated relationship, nor on a fifty-fifty compromise basis, but in a one hundred-one hundred percent compromise arrangement. It is in this overlap of compromise that harmony and beauty are found. Not only is each one refraining from making the other not-OK, but each is actively seeking OKness for the other. This attitude comes into its clearest focus in the act of lovemaking. Sex is sacramental of an intimacy of spirit in which each gives love, security and acceptance to the other, with the end that the other is made to feel OKness.

This kind of marriage requires a relationship with God to operate at its best. The Scriptures make clear that God ordained marriage as an institution within the kingdom of God on earth. When we transplant it into the world, it is out of its native habitat and cannot function as it was intended. Recent statistics show that one out of every three marriages in America ends on the rocks. But among families that attend church regularly the ratio is one out of forty. And among those who pray together each day, the ratio is one out of four hundred.

When both persons have a relationship with God, the Child for each is provided with an OKness that can easily accept the other as OK without the need for You're not-OK. The liberated Adult not only refrains from making the other person not-OK, it actually has the power to attempt to make the other person feel OK. Relating becomes a positive action rather than a negative reaction.

... You're OK with Me

Equipped with this power, the emancipated Adult can in most instances relate in the less than ideal situation—when the other party has a strong not-OK Child. *The secret is in being willing to make the other person feel OK by making him feel superior—even when it makes oneself look inferior—without losing one's own OKness.* This principle is used by many public speakers who make themselves the blunt end of a joke, in effect belittling themselves, in order to make the audience feel OKness at the speaker's expense.

The person who is OK in the universe is in a position to

choose to look inferior in the world for the sake of relating meaningfully to another. The OK-with-God person can accept the not-OK person even with his arrogance, self-centeredness and superficial superiority, because the superiority of another does not affect his own OKness.

This means three things. First, I am willing to accept Hector as he is, not as I would like him to be. I am OK enough to attempt to relate with him as he is, though it may mean maneuvering myself into an inferior position. When Hector comes on strong, I won't let his putting me down get me down. My OKness comes from another source.

Second, I am willing to absorb Hector's offenses against me, to forgive the wrongs he may have either intentionally or inadvertently inflicted on me. I take the hurt and humiliation; I absorb the fallout, the kickback, of his sin against me. My forgiveness is furnished as a perpetual attitude, already available before apology and rectitude.

Recently I heard a person say, "I would just love to forgive Walter—if he would only apologize!" My response was, "Wouldn't we all?" What he was really saying was this: "Walter made me feel not-OK by doing what he did. If he would make himself not-OK by apologizing, I could feel superior enough to be willing to forgive." Then the offender would be absorbing the humiliation, making himself not-OK, and there would be no humiliation left for the offended to absorb. His forgiveness would be cheap and shallow.

I am not suggesting that an Adult-controlled person allows people to push him around. I am saying that he does not allow people to push his attitudes around, and that he does not allow his own reactions to people to push him around. He is OK enough to accept the humiliation and to furnish the forgiveness. His Adult becomes a shock absorber for the kickback of the offense. As *Dear Abby* once said, "Forgiveness is the fragrance of a violet on the heel of the one who crushed it."[1]

When you say, "I'll forgive him, but first I will put him in his place," you are really saying, "I am not big enough (OK enough) to allow him to remain OK. I will accept him only after I have made him little (not-OK)." Your Adult has relinquished its free choice, and you are being push-button-controlled (determined) by a part of you (not-OK Child) which you (Adult) cannot control.

Third, an Adult-controlled person is no longer going to sit in judgment on the offender. The Adult understands that every contributing cause of the offense cannot be known, that all the evidence is not in. An American Indian proverb says, "Never judge another Indian until you have walked six moons in his moccasins."

The Adult understands that we simply do not know enough about the other person. We cannot see far enough into his history to be accurate in our negative evaluation. We are too short-sighted, too near-sighted. We do not know the long road he has trudged or the battle scars he carries. He may have a tack in his shoe that no one on earth knows anything about. Many offenses have been committed and relationships distorted simply because a person had insomnia the night before. We do not know the not-OK feelings recorded in the other person's Child when he was in infancy, over which he had no control.

The Adult-controlled relationship is characterized by the understanding that the other person has a measure of not-OKness in his Child. This understanding enables the Adult to make excuses to himself for the other person.

This is exactly what we see in Jesus. First, he "emptied himself, taking the form of a servant" (Phil. 2:7). The Authorized Version puts it even more plainly: "He made himself of no reputation." Jesus was OK enough to become "inferior." Then, "When he was reviled, he did not revile in return; when he suffered, he did not threaten; but he trusted himself to him who judges justly" (1 Pet. 2:23). His relationship with God gave him an OKness that needed no props or ego defenses. Then on the cross he looked with sympathetic eyes out over the multitude whose brutal act of barbaric terrorism was crushing his own life, and said, "Father, forgive them; for they know not what they do" (Lk. 23:34). He saw their vicious, beastly act through eyes of sympathy and made to himself an excuse for them. He saw their not-OK Child, and he himself was so OK that he absorbed the world's most hostile, heinous crime without retaliation.

There are many Hectors—unloved, unattractive and unwanted persons so not-OK that only those with a Christlike OKness can relate to them. Only those with an Adult that accepts, forgives and understands sympathetically at the cost of humiliation and inferiority can provide for the unlovely an OKness for meaningful relationships.

When I'm OK with God, then You're OK with me.

12

LOVE IN ACTION

*T*he most abused word in our language is *love*. It has been so degraded and cheapened that everything from jealousy to lust now passes for love. Marriages are crumbling and human relationships are breaking apart because they are being built on a counterfeit.

The Counterfeit and the Real Thing
As an imitation of the genuine, any counterfeit resembles the authentic on surface, but it completely fails to duplicate its essential quality. Imitation love attracts two persons together, but unlike the genuine it cannot hold them together. It offers happiness, but the commercial is phony and true happiness is never delivered. It offers a personality-interaction, but there is more reaction than responsiveness because it is based on getting rather than giving. It is self-centered instead of other-centered, conscious of being loved rather than loving, receiving rather than giving.

Counterfeit love is a noun, sort of a depository for love received. Authentic love is a verb, characterized primarily by commitment, by giving out. It is the difference between longing to be accepted and a willingness to accept, between the pleasure of being pleased and the pleasure of pleasing, between the desire to be served and the willingness to serve. The one wants to be made OK, and the other is preoccupied with making the other OK.

The functional difference between the counterfeit and the authentic is seen in the difference between the Child and Adult. The Child needs to be loved. Bellevue Hospital in New York City has organized "Love Volunteers" who come in to sing and to rock the babies. Everybody has a Child that needs to receive love, but the need to be loved is not love. When the need to be loved is substituted for love, it becomes at best an imitation.

Neither successful marriages nor harmonious human relationships can be structured alone on the need to be loved. Two persons attempting to build a life together on the basis of a common need only compound the problem unless built into the arrangement is a mutual fulfillment of the need.

The economics of love require an equalization of production and consumption. Today we have a need-and-supply problem—we have a surplus of persons with a Child that needs love and a deficit of persons with an Adult to provide the love. Thus we have an economic depression. People are starving for love, so they substitute domestic arrangements and live-in privileges. They are not equipped with an Adult to return love for love, so they offer the only thing they have—passion. Consequently, the price of love has hit rock bottom and love has become dirt cheap.

When each person has an adequate Adult to supply the love to satisfy the need of the other's Child, the Child-need is not mistaken for Adult-love and it therefore poses no problem. The Child's need for love is actually necessary in that it makes the partner's Adult love wanted, thus holding the couple together in an interlocking, interacting companionship. Each person's Adult gives love to the other's Child, and each person's Child receives love from the other's Adult. The Child's need for love is not a counterfeit need; it is a genuine need. It is only counterfeit when it replaces love, in the same way that play money is all right for playing and becomes counterfeit only when it is passed as U.S. dollars.

Love and the Need for Recognition

The not-OK Child also has other needs, the fulfillment of which is often mistaken for love. The Child needs recognition, the security of importance, the OKness of being "somebody special."

Judy, who needs security, feels complimented when John, a star athlete, asks her for a date. She is flattered by his invitation and feels a kind of OKness from his interest. She feels she is "somebody special" to someone whom the public considers somebody special. When she is with John, Judy feels like a queen. Her Child's need for OKness has been met.

This is all well and good—until Judy mistakes her feeling of OKness with John for an Adult love for John. Instead of loving John, so far she only loves being flattered by John and feeling "somebody special" by being with him. She is directing love toward herself and is not yet prepared to give

Adult love to John. The value of this feeling that attracts Judy to John need not be minimized, because it can often lead to authentic love. But when it is mistaken for Adult love, it is counterfeit. The arrangement that holds the relationship together is inadequate.

John also has a not-OK Child that needs the security of recognition and distinction. Judy's willingness to be dominated gives him a possessive feeling of ownership. He feels he is really "somebody" to have a girl like Judy. He is drawn to Judy by the OKness his Child gets from being with her. And he mistakes his feeling of OKness with Judy for an Adult love for Judy. Instead of loving Judy, so far he only loves feeling like "somebody" when he is with Judy. What is considered love is the counterfeit love of a substitute, the noun of a feeling rather than the verb of in-action loving.

Up to this point the OKness that Judy and John receive from each other may remain through a lifetime to *help* their marriage function, but when it is mistaken for love it is counterfeit and will never sustain the relationship.

Loved by God

When the Child's need for the security of importance is fulfilled by being accepted by God, the Child gets the feeling of being "somebody special" in the universe. An OKness is gained from the relationship with God that transcends the OKness from any other relationship on earth.

When this existential need for importance in the universe is not OKed, an exaggerated self-love builds up as arrogance and self-centeredness. Judy may fall in love with her mirror and John with his exploits. Feeling worthless and not-OK in the universe, their not-OK feelings in the world are intensified. The desire to become "somebody special" becomes overwhelming, and the Child becomes uncontrollable. Judy and John become desperate for each other. The contaminated Adult loses its capacity for authentic love, and its ability to distinguish between the imitation and the real is diminished.

The relationship with God does not remove the need for meaningful relationships with other persons, and an OKness in the universe does not eliminate the need for OKness in the world. The person who is OK with God still has a Child that needs the love and recognition of other persons. What the God-relationship does is to give an OKness in a bigger context than the world, thus decontaminating the Adult from the exaggerated, overwhelming self-centeredness of the Child. The emancipated Adult becomes free to be in command over the Child's not-OKness in the world. The Child's need for love and importance in the world is controllable because the greater need for love and importance in the universe is satisfied. And the Adult is in a position to understand the difference between the Child's need and an Adult love.

Another obstruction to Adult love stems from the You're not-OK attitude of the Child that has become arrogant and self-centered. The person who is so not-OK that he builds his own false OKness by making the other person not-OK soon comes to hate those he considers not-OK—especially those who refuse to accept the inferiority they have been assigned. It should go without being said that Child hate and Adult love are mutually exclusive.

When the relationship with God makes my Child OK in the universe, there is no need for You're not-OK to bolster my OKness. When I am really OK, you become OK to me. You're not-OK is removed from my Child, allowing the hate to dissolve and making room for my Adult love.

Another source of hate is the guilt the Parent produces in the Child. When a person or situation is faced inadequately, an emotional equation is set up. The inadequate response to the person prompts the Parent to accuse, thus producing guilt in the Child. When the guilt is not handled correctly it brings on fear, and fear leads to hate. A white person feels guilty because he does not love a black person. His guilt makes him fear black people. Then he begins to hate them. The Adult is contaminated with Child hate, and Adult love cannot operate.

In a relationship with God the sin is erased and the guilt dissolved. The Child feels the security of acceptance and forgiveness. Guilt gone, the fear and hate are overcome. And Adult love can function.

Love Is a Four-Letter Verb

In this chapter I have shown how the Adult is emancipated from the contamination that precludes authentic love. What then is genuine love, and how is it gained?

In one of Schulz' *Peanuts* strips, Linus wants to be a doctor when he grows up. Lucy, in her typically sarcastic way, says, "You can't be a doctor. You don't love mankind enough." To which Linus reacts, "I love mankind; it's people I can't stand!"

This depicts the difference between an idealistic, visionary, counterfeit love and a realistic, acting, authentic love. The Scripture says, "For God so loved . . . that he gave . . ." (Jn. 3:16). "Christ loved the church and gave himself up for her" (Eph. 5:25). The essence of Adult love is giving—the verb, love in action. (Though love is the *function* of the Nurturing Parent, I am calling genuine love "Adult" because it is *chosen* by the Adult.) *Adult love has no necessary connection with Child feeling.* If love is action, and action is a matter of Adult choice, then *a person can love whomever he freely chooses to love.* Love is not something that grabs you; it is something that you choose to grab. The love that sustains a relationship is a voluntary choice on the part of the Adult after examining the options. I am not saying the Child's needs should not be considered in choosing a mate, but I am saying that an Adult willingness to love when the romance is gone is the only adequate ingredient that will hold a relationship.

The Adult choice to love is the choice to absorb the irritations that threaten the relationship, the choice to keep love in forward gear when circumstances have reversed themselves, to make oneself the goat when necessary to preserve the relationship, and to keep loving (verb) when the love (noun, feeling) is static.

The greatest love act ever witnessed took place on a hill called Calvary. In that act of love I cannot discover a visionary, romantic sentimentality, but I see the most dangerous, most daring, most costly love in world history. Jesus was not the helpless victim of a love that possessed him; he was the voluntary victim of a love he had chosen. To choose to love is to make oneself vulnerable to the object of the love. It includes a reckless abandonment of self-interests in the nitty-gritty of life and a willingness to sacrifice for the interests of the loved. Authentic love is tough!

Adult love is not the drooling sentimentality of two teenagers under the moonlight, but an old man stroking the hand of a wife whose body is wasting away with malignancy and saying, "You are more beautiful to me now than when you wore your wedding dress."

This Adult-chosen love helps insulate one's own Child from the offenses that occur in human relationships, and it lubricates those relationships for smooth functioning. And this Adult-chosen love has carried numerous couples beyond the golden anniversary with a dynamic which novel fantasy could never generate and has given them a joy that transcends the fleeting thrills of romance.

This kind of loving is available for those who have an OK-with-God Child and an Adult that is emancipated from exaggerated self-love and shored up by a relationship with God.

13

THE ADULT IN CONTROL

*T*he list is endless. A relationship with God will not make every area of life automatically victorious, but it frees the Adult from the not-OK Child and empowers the Adult to choose appropriately.

OK in the Face of Temptation, Temper and Failure
Let's look first at temptation. There are three stages to most temptations: the evil suggestion, the period of pondering and the moment of yielding. The battle against the temptation is not nearly so difficult as the battle against something inside me which responds to the temptation. The temptation does not take hold of me; something within me latches onto the suggestion, grips it and will not let it go. This inner something is the Child's desire to experience what has been suggested.

The Child response is usually minimal during the first stage of the suggestion (unless a consistent habit of yielding to the particular temptation has been formed). The real problem comes during stage two when the suggestion is taken in for consideration. During this period of pondering the imagination works overtime, the suggestion accumulates fantasy and often even becomes an obsession. By this time the Child's response has contaminated the Adult, and the suggestion becomes virtually irresistible. The Child so tightly grips the suggestion that the Adult cannot shake loose. The Adult is enslaved to the suggestion by the Child that was allowed to grow to uncontrollable proportions. The Adult is contaminated and deactivated by the Child.

The liberated Adult understands the liability of being recontaminated by the Child and therefore is in a position to refuse to be maneuvered into such a position of vulnerability. The Adult chooses its own battleground, calls its own signals and specifies its own terms. The secret of successfully overcoming temptation is called "nipping it in the bud," surrendering the suggestion before it reaches the period of pondering. The Adult never stops to listen to the sales pitch; it occupies the mind with opposite thoughts; it remains in a free position of command. The secret is not in being *strong* enough to overcome the temptation but in being *positioned* to overcome.

A second problem area is temper, which properly belongs to the Child. Here again the secret is not in being strong enough to control the temper but in being positioned to command the Child. The remedy is not to sit on the lid to keep it from exploding but to be in a position to quit refueling the flames that cause the steam buildup. The Adult chooses carefully its point of attack, not doing battle with temper but with the causes of temper. The Child that is suppressed by the Adult causes ulcers. The Child that is offered OKness by the Adult is without the need of a tantrum. Instead of holding the Child down, the Adult turns off the Child recordings.

A third problem is human failure. We stumble so often and fall on our little beat-up faces. The Child feels discouragement, defeat and not-OKness. The Parent becomes accusatorial and whips the Child with feelings of guilt.

The emancipated Adult can quickly move to control the situation. The Parent is given appropriate content for the particular situation, thus eliminating false guilt. The Adult turns on the Child's OK-with-God recordings to overcome the discouragement. The circumstances of the failure may not be changed, but the Child has other recordings to respond to. When computed by the Adult, the OK-with-God feelings outplay the not-OK feelings of failure. And the Adult can examine the circumstance of the failure so that the meaning of the failure is changed from defeat to challenge.

OK in the Face of Dishonesty and Disappointment

Fourth, many persons wrestle with the problem of a creeping, insidious dishonesty. Unreality is fabricated as a smoke screen to hide the reality of not-OKness. Sometimes the dishonesty takes the form of an ostrich with a head buried in the sand. Our world is being threatened by poverty, exploitation, prejudice and alarming forces that could destroy freedom. It causes both guilt and fear in the Child, so he switches his mental television set to another channel and refuses to expose himself to the needs of the world. A heavy smoker became disturbed every time he read an article in the *Reader's Digest* about the harmful effects of smoking. So he decided to quit—reading the *Reader's Digest*!

Playhouses are built and games of make-believe are played. Fictitious castles of pretension are erected to shelter oneself from the reality of himself. A man refuses to ask what the other is talking about for fear he might expose his own ignorance. So he keeps nodding his head as if he understands perfectly. He listens to the telling of a joke and laughs before the punch line for fear someone will think he did not understand. A son is not doing well in school and the blame is placed on the teacher. Not-OKness is fabricated for the other person as a psychological hideout to escape the exposure of one's own not-OKness.

The person who is OK in the universe has a confidence that allows inferiority in the world. The Adult is freed to admit the not-OK feelings of the Child because the OKness in the universe will not be affected. What other persons think about you becomes less important than what God knows about you. You can own yourself as you are without having to prop up and protect your self-image with pretensions. What a great feeling it is to let your entire weight down on what you really are, knowing you are resting on something adequate to hold you!

A fifth problem is disappointment. Dreams burst like bubbles in the air, hopes are buried, faith is shattered, ambitions are broken. The goal you hitched your life to suddenly seems impossible, and you are left grasping at straws.

Only the person with the God-relationship can see the "here and now" from the standpoint of the "out there and beyond," the present in the light of the future, the disconcerting things of life in relation to God and eternity. Underlying the changing, the relative, the short-lived, the not-OKness in the world, he catches a feel of the permanent, the timeless, the absolute, the OKness in the universe. He still has everything when he has nothing else. His life is anchored.

OK in the Face of Death

Lastly, someday everyone is going to check out of the human race—and face the phenomenon of death. That final moment of life is going to wrap everything up. Misplaced values will be straightened out. Priorities will be altered. The values that had seemed so important will be worthless then, and those that had been least important will be monumental. All the OKness in the world will be like ashes in the mouth, and all the not-OKness in the world will be stripped of its anguish. The only thing that will matter then is an OKness with God. At that moment those who are OK in the universe are a part of the "in group" in eternity.

Thomas Harris writes of the traumatic experience of the fetus during the process of birth.[1] The baby is accustomed to the intimacy, warmth and OKness of the womb world, a world that is small enough to support it emotionally. Suddenly it is thrust out into a world of devastating contrasts of cold and heat and light and darkness. For a short time the infant is cut off and detached. But within moments the baby is taken by loving hands and wrapped in a blanket, and it discovers there is someone "out there."

Unknown to the unborn baby in its smaller world, it really belonged to a bigger world. Provision was already being made for its debut. Even before it was born it was accepted by parents, family and friends. It was OK in its womb world, but the infant was also OK in advance in the real world.

Man makes adjustments to feel security in his relationships in the world, but so many fail to realize they belong to the universe. And they are confronted with anxieties when they face the unknown of that bigger "world." Death becomes a catastrophic, traumatic experience.

Those persons, however, who are OK with God soon discover Someone "out there" in that unknown. An Old Testament writer said, "The eternal God is your dwelling place, and underneath are the everlasting arms" (Deut. 33:27). And the psalmist sang, "Though I walk through the valley of the shadow of death . . . , Thou art with me" (Ps. 23:4).

Those in the world who have a relationship with God are already OK in the universe. For them, death will be like birth into a larger reality, and all the not-OKness in the world will then seem trivial.

FOOTNOTES

Chapter 1
[1]*Aids to Reflection.*
[2]Thomas A. Harris, *I'm OK–You're OK* (New York: Avon Books, 1969), p. 210.
[3]Ibid., p. 190.
[4]Ibid., p. 201.
[5]From *The Twentieth Century New Testament.*

Chapter 2
[1]B. P. Dotsenko, "From Communism to Christianity," *Christianity Today,* January 5, 1973, p. 5.
[2]Alfred North Whitehead, *The Function of Reason* (Boston: Beacon Press, 1958), pp. 4-5, 29.

Chapter 3
[1]Shakespeare, *Hamlet,* Act II, Scene 2.
[2]Quoted in Ralph Harper, *The Seventh Solitude* (Baltimore: The Johns Hopkins Press, 1965), p. 12.

[3]Quoted in Billy Graham, *The Challenge* (Garden City: Doubleday, 1969), p. 37.
[4]Clare Booth Luce, "What Really Killed Marilyn Monroe," *Reader's Digest*, November, 1964.

Chapter 4
[1]Richard Hooker, *Ecclesiastical Polity*, Bk. I, Ch. 2.
[2]C. S. Lewis, *Surprised by Joy* (New York: Harcourt, Brace and Company, 1955), p. 229.

Chapter 7
[1]Harris, p. 261.

Chapter 11
[1]Abigail VanBuren, "Dear Abby," *The Lexington Leader*, Lexington, Kentucky, October 8, 1973, p. 19.

Chapter 13
[1]Harris, pp. 63-64.